"*Breathing Room* is a fascinating blend of the spiritual, practical, and personal stories... provides a clear guide to accomplish the inner work you need to do not only to declutter your physical world but also to accomplish this in mind and spirit."
—**Matt Chan**, creator and executive producer

breathing room

Open Your Heart
by decluttering your home

LAUREN ROSENFELD + DR. MELVA GREEN

Advance Praise for
breathing room

"With clarity, compassion, and humor, Lauren Rosenfeld and Dr. Melva Green help us see the deep connection between living space and heart space—guiding us toward freedom and ease within both. With both spiritual lessons and easy to do exercises, this book is a perfect blend of theory and practice. Readers of *Breathing Room* will soon find themselves rejoicing in the wide-open spaces of both home and heart."

—Joan Borysenko, PhD, author of
Minding the Body, Mending the Mind and
Inner Peace for Busy People

"*Breathing Room* puts the om into your home and the grease into your elbows! This is where the spirituality of clutter meets practicality with a big dose of compassion. Well done!"

—Tisha Morris, author of *Mind Body Home*

"*Breathing Room* is a fascinating blend of the spiritual, practical, and personal stories about how we can all declutter our lives. The book provides a clear guide to accomplishing the inner work you need to do not only to declutter your physical world but also to accomplish this in mind and spirit."

—Matt Chan, creator and executive producer
of the A&E series *Hoarders*

"This book is genius. If you shut down when faced with your clutter, if clutter is stopping you from living the beautiful life that is your birthright, read this book! It has what you need to change your relationship to clutter forever!"

—**Jennifer Louden**, author of
The Woman's Comfort Book
and *The Life Organizer*

"Who knew that clearing your physical space of unnecessary clutter could be a path of self-reflection and deep learning? Well Lauren Rosenfeld and Dr. Melva Green, that's who! In *Breathing Room*, these two wise women guide us in how to learn from the spaces where we live and create rooms that reflect a nourished and nourishing heart. With compassion and humor they help us find a way to let the beauty we are shine through the inevitable messiness of being human."

—**Oriah Mountain Dreamer**,
author of *The Invitation*

"A compassionate guide to clearing out your clutter and inviting space, light, and peace into your home and heart."

—**Francine Jay**, author of
The Joy of Less, A Minimalist Living Guide

breathing
room

breathing room

Open Your Heart
by decluttering your home

LAUREN ROSENFELD + DR. MELVA GREEN

ATRIA PAPERBACK
New York London Toronto Sydney New Delhi

BEYOND WORDS
Hillsboro, Oregon

ATRIA PAPERBACK
A Division of Simon & Schuster, Inc.
1230 Avenue of the Americas
New York, NY 10020

BEYOND WORDS
20827 N.W. Cornell Road, Suite 500
Hillsboro, Oregon 97124-9808
503-531-8700 / 503-531-8773 fax
www.beyondword.com

Managing editor: Lindsay S. Brown
Editors: Gretchen Stelter, Anna Noak, Emmalisa Sparrow
Copyeditor: Claire Rudy Foster
Proofreader: Linda Meyer
Design: Devon Smith
Composition: William H. Brunson Typography Services

First Atria Paperback/Beyond Words trade paperback edition April 2014

For information about special discounts for bulk purchases, please contact Simon & Schuster Special Sales at 1-866-506-1949 or business@simonandschuster.com.

The Simon & Schuster Speakers Bureau can bring authors to your live event. For more information or to book an event, contact the Simon & Schuster Speakers Bureau at 1-866-248-3049 or visit our website at www.simonspeakers.com.

Manufactured in the United States of America

10 9 8 7 6 5 4 3 2 1

Library of Congress Cataloging-in-Publication Data

Rosenfeld, Lauren.
   Breathing room : open your heart by decluttering your home / Lauren Rosenfeld and Dr. Melva Green. — First Atria Paperback/Beyond Words trade paperback edition.
      p. cm.
      1. Spiritual life. 2. Orderliness—Miscellanea. 3. Storage in the home—Miscellanea.
   I. Title.
   BL624.R67   2014
   646.7—dc23

                                                                        2013041861

ISBN 978-1-58270-457-9
ISBN 978-1-4767-3946-5 (ebook)

The corporate mission of Beyond Words Publishing, Inc.: *Inspire to Integrity*

For Jamie,
whose love is a treasure that shines on the
mantel of my heart.

—LR

For JB,
whose Divine presence ignites the
remembrance in me that I was born to fly.

—MG

Contents

Preface   xiii

Introduction: How We Can Help You, Your Home,
and Your Heart   xix

1. The Nature of Clutter   1

Step One: Stop and Listen

2. Stop   21
3. Listen   25

Step Two: Intend

4. Intend   37
5. Your Home Entry: Room for Open Invitation   49
6. Your Living Room: Room for Relaxation and Happiness   55
7. Your Dining Room: Room for Nourishment and Sharing   65
8. Your Kitchen: Room for Collaboration and Creativity   71
9. Your Child's Room: Room for Growth and Change   79
10. Your Home Office: Room for Information
and Inspiration   91
11. Your Bedroom: Room for Rest and Love   101
12. Your Bathroom: Room for Self-Acceptance and Renewal   111
13. Your Storage: Room for Life-Giving Memories   121

14. Your Breathing Room: Room for Mindfulness
    and Compassion   131

Step Three: Clear the Energy

15. The Ten Principles of Spiritual Decluttering   141
16. Principle 1: Don't Attack—Clear with Compassion   143
17. Principle 2: Out with Consuming Emotions,
    In with Sustainable Emotions   155
18. Principle 3: Letting Go with Grace and Gratitude   167
19. Principle 4: Accept Where You Are   179
20. Principle 5: Just Say No to Clutter Enablers
    and Clutter Dumps   187
21. Principle 6: Pass Your Clutter Through the
    Three Gates of Meaning   203
22. Principle 7: The Three Standards of True Value—
    Happiness, Freedom, Ease   213
23. Principle 8: Consider Your Legacy as You Live   223
24. Principle 9: No More Hiding Places   239
25. Principle 10: Your Home Is Already Uncluttered—
    It Is in Its Nature to Be That Way   249

A Final Note: Embracing the Sacred Messiness of Life   255
Acknowledgments   259

Preface

We knew from the start that we were soul sisters: two women—a medical doctor and a spiritual intuitive—both on winding and wondrous life paths, stepping with mindful gratitude in our work, while managing the innumerable details of our families. The two of us just got each other. And that was all we needed to know.

We are both mothers running households, so we understand how important having a decluttered home is to freeing up space in the heart for spiritual freedom. Lauren is a married mother of four active and imaginative teenagers, who are wildly creative clutter-producing maniacs. She lives in the heart of a spiritual mecca in the Blue Ridge Mountains, where the buzz of cars and the sound of bongo drums and strumming guitars are constant companions. Lauren is a spiritual declutterer: an intuitive guide who helps clients see the spiritual lessons shining in their natural messiness. She offers help to clients who feel overwhelmed with the business (and busyness) of life and helps them see that within every struggle is a miracle waiting to be born.

Dr. Melva Green is a single mother with one beloved son who is a born philosopher and gifted musician. She travels between the broad and wild beaches of Costa Rica and the cultural and intellectual feast that is Berkeley, California. She is a board-certified psychiatrist who is best known for her role on A&E's hit show *Hoarders*, where her compassionate care, forthright advice, and brave willingness to combine the science of her professional training with the intuition of spirit have endeared her to clients and television viewers alike.

Lauren's Story

In the summer of 2009, I had the privilege and honor of going with my husband and four children on retreat with author, poet, Zen master, and peace activist Thich Nhat Hanh. On the second day of the retreat, he delivered a talk about creating a "breathing room"— a room that serves as a retreat within the home for seeking peace, solace, compassion, and reconciliation. "In the twenty-first century," he said, "every home needs such a room." And he began to talk about how such a room could be created. And he was talking to me. Literally. It was not *as if* he was talking to me. He was actually looking at me—and I felt that he was telling me to go home and create a breathing room.

I went home with that sacred intention: to create a room for peace and compassion. The trouble was, there was no spare room in my home. Every room, closet, and storage space was in use. I knew that in order to find space for a breathing room in my house, I needed to remove some of our belongings. I needed to declutter.

The task seemed very simple and straightforward until I came to the deepest emotional layer of clutter: the stuff that stopped me in my tracks. Mind you, I knew I needed to let go of these things, but I physically could not release them. These objects represented deep emotional attachments for me. They did not bring me any joy. On the contrary, they made me feel terrible—queasy and burdened. Making a decision about them made my head spin.

I came to see that though I said I valued and longed for freedom, peace, and compassion, I was choosing fear over happiness by allowing my clutter to occupy my breathing room. I was choosing my emotional attachments over my spiritual freedom. That is when I chose to look at each piece of physical clutter as an opportunity to look at the emotional clutter that was preventing my spiritual growth. As I decluttered my home, what I loved and valued stood out more clearly—emotionally and physically. Through that experience, I learned that decluttering is a spiritual process that involves coming into communion with what is truly important.

When I shared this with friends and family, they had so many questions: How do I let go of objects that cause so much stress and strain? How do I overcome the resistance and fear I experience when I try to declutter? How do I manage the overwhelm and exhaustion?

I saw that the need to declutter at every level of our being—physically, mentally, emotionally, and spiritually—was deep-seated in many people and that these people needed a guide. They needed a book that not only helped them see the connections to the clutter we keep inside and the clutter that manifests outwardly, but that gave compassionate encouragement to do the work of liberating space, and offered exercises to make that work joyful and sustainable.

I did not realize as I was imagining this book that soul healer, physician, television personality, and all-around sassy Southern belle—my sister in spirit, Dr. Melva Green—was undergoing her own transformative process of decluttering her life and finding a different kind of breathing room that required her to leave behind a successful traditional psychiatric practice in the United States in order to find her authentic voice as a holistic healer.

Melva's Story

From the outside looking in, my life was perfect. As a Johns Hopkins-trained, board-certified psychiatrist, I'd been through all the rigors that are required of Western medical practitioners. I've had my own private practice, offered private therapy sessions, made medical referrals, and written prescriptions. I had all the accolades and prestige that come from years of devotion to my craft. I had the respect of colleagues and the attention of the media. But inside, I felt like an imposter, living someone else's dream. From childhood, I have been a spiritual intuitive. I was born with a persistent inner voice guiding me to see the inner life that dwells within all human beings. Yet that voice, powerful as it was, was not what I considered the call to worldly success. So I dampened that voice. I pushed it down and proceeded down the career path clearly laid out before me—I felt I would risk everything by letting my inner voice out.

At the time, I lived in a beautiful home that I shared with my son. He was perfectly content, but I was anything but. Though I was surrounded by people who loved and respected me, deep down I felt completely alone. One day, I felt I could no longer live a lie. How could I continue to nurture my son when I could not nurture myself? What good was my career when I felt that I was shrinking inside? So I made a decision that most people would consider crazy: I closed the practice I had worked so hard to build. I left the beautiful home that I had paid for with the proceeds of my practice and moved to Costa Rica, where I would have the breathing room to rediscover myself and reinvent my life. I let go of everything I knew in order to discover everything I needed to know.

I deliberately moved to a home where the electronic connections I had previously valued were hard to find. Phone lines were frequently down. If I wanted to use the internet, I had to trudge through a rainforest to get to the closest town. Once I was away from people constantly having access to me, I finally found my breathing room. I had space—pure, open space. All I had to do was mother and meditate. With these two practices, I got to the work of finding breathing room. I opened every dark space within myself and took honest inventory of what I had been holding inside for years. In the process, I went deeper into those internal spaces than I had ever gone before.

So imagine my surprise when, in the midst of this life transition, the popular A&E show *Hoarders* called me. At that time, they were in their fifth season, with traditionally trained therapists. I thought the full disclosure of my spiritual solution for healing anxiety conditions, hoarding syndrome, and other behavioral disorders would send them running for the hills. But it had just the opposite effect. They loved it! It was, in their words, "refreshing, exciting, and engaging." They were right—and the viewers felt the same way.

One of those viewers, my beautiful soul sister Lauren Rosenfeld, contacted me about a book she was writing called *Breathing Room*. She wanted feedback because of my involvement with *Hoarders*. She had no idea how deeply I connected with the idea of breathing room and how finding that room in my own inner life had completely transformed me. I knew instantly that this project would offer people a process for the inner work that I had found so liberating. I wanted to offer readers the same sense of freedom and inner divinity that I had found when I created breathing room in my life.

So when Lauren asked me if the creation of *Breathing Room* was a journey I wanted to embark upon with her, my answer was, "Oh, hell yes! Get your butt down to Costa Rica and let's do this!"

So we met. Lauren flew to Costa Rica, where a bus spewing powerful diesel fumes bumped down a rutted road and dropped her off at my doorstep, dust covered, sweaty, and smiling. We two soul sisters (and now coauthors) embraced. I took her into town for a refreshing drink of coconut water straight from a green coconut, and the two of us began to imagine how our two voices could come together to change hearts, homes, families, and lives.

Our two journeys merged to become a single strand that unites Melva's years of experience as a psychiatrist (and lifelong calling to spiritual healing) with Lauren's passion for helping people engage with the spiritual depths of their daily lives. In the course of writing this book, our path has taken us to meet declutterers whose stories you will encounter throughout this book. It is our hope that through these stories, our reflections on them, and the exercises we suggest, you'll find your own path—a path which slices through your clutter and leads you to the open spaces within your home and your heart: your breathing room.

Introduction:
How We Can Help You,
Your Home, and Your Heart

In the pages of this book, we will help you look deeply at the clutter in your home so you can see that, just beneath the clutter, illuminating spiritual lessons and emotional ah-has are waiting to help you not only liberate space in your home but also space in your heart, as well as give flight to your spirit and rock your world.

In these pages, you will find not only advice from a medical doctor and a spiritual intuitive, but you will also find case studies of people just like yourself, people who struggle with clutter in their homes and their hearts and who want to free themselves of this clutter but simply don't know where to begin. We set them on the path by making one connection clear: your heart is like a home. The home is like a heart. And you, my friend, can make both places open, light-filled, and a joy to reside in.

But first, it's important for us to note that the way to freedom is not always simple. In this process, history, perception, and emotion are intricately intertwined. It's a complex journey each person must undertake with compassion and self-awareness. While certain exercises, models, and tools can be helpful, individuals have different emotions that link them to their past and different possessions that they may need to hold on to in order to properly heal. It may take time to revel in memory and love before we can release what needs to go—if it needs to go at all. Not everything can simply be sliced away because we do not see the purpose of it; you will decide for yourself what can stay and what should go. This is your personal journey and only you know how to make that journey safe and comfortable.

A Note from Dr. Green on the Nature of Tough Love and Transformation

Compassion takes many forms. Some people have said that I have a tough love approach. One fan of *Hoarders* once told me, "You know, Dr. Green, you're like this perfect harmonic balance between empathy, compassion, love, and 'C'mon now! Get your shit straight!'"

I actually don't consider myself to be tough at all. I consider myself to be to be a spiritual midwife who is trained as a psychiatrist. When a client is going through a significant transformation, it is like being in labor. A miracle is about to happen—but if something goes wrong, we have to get the baby and the mother out of distress. If the person undergoing transformation is in a "spiritual labor" crisis, I can't be sweet or gentle in that moment.

I consider it my role to aid people as they get to the next stage of their spiritual and emotional birthing process. I can't let nature take its course when time is of the essence and someone's life is at risk. In those cases, being gentle is not the most appropriate form of compassion. It does not honor the reality of the situation. And as any *Hoarders* fan might tell you, I will always be honest, because without honesty, transformation is not possible.

How to Read and Use this Book

This spiritual method of decluttering can be summarized in one word: SLICE. This is an acronym for *Stop and Listen. Intend. Clear the Energy*. This method is the most powerful way to cut through clutter in your home and your heart to reveal the shining truth and beauty underneath.

Lauren uses this method with her private clients, and it is so easy and effective, that when followed as we detail in this book, the clutter practically removes itself.

The SLICE method is a holistic approach to decluttering. If you declutter your home without doing the same for your heart, you are carrying around emotional clutter and will not be able to be present in your decluttered home. If you declutter your heart without decluttering your relationships, you will quickly find yourself drawn into conflict (or conflict avoidance) that will fill your heart back up with anger, guilt, and resentment. If you declutter your home, your heart, and your relationships without attending to your roles and responsibilities, you will find yourself so exhausted and burned out that you can't find the energy to enjoy your life. This is about taking care of it all—making room within it all. With our process, gorgeous, elemental Divine light can cascade through every aspect of your life and your work in the world.

There are three steps to the SLICE method.

The First Step: Stop and Listen

Even though *Stop and Listen* may sound like the easiest step, it is the most challenging, because we are asking you to change your habits of being. You have to stop running away from your clutter and listen to the lesson it's trying to teach you. Yet the impulse to run is strong in all of us. In fact, sometimes this impulse may feel overpowering. Recently, Lauren was at a dinner party when one of the guests remarked, "I don't know how you do what you do." When Lauren asked why, he answered, "Just looking at clutter makes me nervous. It makes me want to run."

He's not alone. Clutter makes us want to run for the hills—but not for the reasons we think. It's not just because it's messy (which, of course, it is) and it's not just because it's time consuming (which, of course, it is). It's because of what the clutter represents to us: our history, fears, worries, and uncomfortable and painful emotions.

The first step of the SLICE process is to slow down and look at your clutter mindfully. Our physical clutter is simply a manifestation of the emotional clutter we carry inside. If we attempt to remove the physical clutter without consciously acknowledging the emotional clutter it represents, then two things might happen. First, we might resist decluttering altogether because of the natural urge to turn away from our painful feelings. Second, we may find that even if we have the courage to remove the clutter, if we don't mindfully and compassionately acknowledge our feelings, the physical clutter will return, because the emotions that caused the clutter want and need to be acknowledged and will manifest as physical clutter again and again until we do so. In the first step, we also introduce you to the emotions that tend to generate clutter and teach you how to loosen their hold on your heart.

The Second Step: Intend

In the second section, *Intend*, we will examine each room's emotional and spiritual significance. You will be challenged to look at rooms as more than just spaces that house your furniture; they are an outward manifestation of your emotional and spiritual life. For each space, you will pick at least three words to describe the energy that you want to create in that particular room. You will make signs to serve as a reminder of your intention for creating energies in each room. We also suggest you create a decluttering journal. Whether you choose a beautiful hardbound journal with a decorative cover or a simple spiral bound notebook does not matter. Just keep it accessible so that you are able to record your thoughts as you go through your decluttering journey.

You may find that not every room we mention applies to your home. Even so, we suggest that you spend some time reading each section, because even though you may not have certain physical rooms in your home, you do have analogous spaces in your heart. For example, you may live in an apartment with no formal entry hall or foyer, but you do have a space in your heart for open invitation. Or, you may live in a home without a dining room, but you still have the need for emotional nourishment and sharing that this space represents.

You may like to read these chapters in order, but it is not necessary to do that. You can read them in the order that will help you feel most comfortable. Some people may find that they would like to begin by exploring the room that holds the least amount of clutter and build up to the room with the most. Others might find that they would rather go directly to the room that is most cluttered; having created space there, they move on to rooms that feel emotionally and physically lighter. Use your intuition to guide you, and work in the order that feels most comfortable.

The Third Step: Clear the Energy

In the third section of the book, *Clear the Energy*, we will go over the Ten Principles of Spiritual Decluttering. Once you have set your intention, you can understand more deeply how you will go about clearing out the possessions that do not resonate with the energy you intend for your rooms. With each of these principles, you will find an exercise for decluttering your home, your heart, your relationships, and your roles and responsibilities. With the completion of each exercise, you will feel just how liberating it is to SLICE through the clutter that has been binding your home and heart.

For each of the principles, there are four exercises: one each for decluttering your home, your heart, your relationships, and your roles and responsibilities. Though it is not necessary to do these exercises in any specific order, we suggest that you read through and understand each of the ten principles before you jump into the exercises, since some of them may speak more clearly to your heart than others. For example, you may find that the fourth principle, "Accept where you are," speaks powerfully to where you are in your life's path because you have been longing for complete and compassionate acceptance. Or maybe you are drawn to the principle "Consider your legacy as you live" because you might be contemplating what is most important to pass on to the generations that follow you.

Once you understand all of these principles, you will know best where to begin. We suggest that once you choose a principle, you do all four exercises associated with that principle. This way, you can come to see the power of this decluttering principle and its power to create breathing room in your heart, your home, your relationships, and your time.

In the final section of the book, *Embracing the Sacred Messiness of Life*, we will give you the wisdom you need to stay decluttered. Decluttering is not a do-it-once-and-never-do-it-again activity. It is an attitude, a way of seeing, a way of being in the world.

Throughout this book, you will meet some of our actual clients. As you read their stories, you'll find out just what they were running from and the spiritual lessons they gained when they had the courage to stop and listen, intend, and clear the energy. Our hope is that you may recognize something of yourself in them. Perhaps their situations aren't precisely like yours. Maybe the kinds of clutter they've accumulated are different from yours, but we guarantee that their fears, worries, and regrets will strike a chord with you. We are all human beings—we all experience the emotions that lead us to clutter our homes and hearts. You will read how Lauren helped each client to spiritually declutter, and you'll get Dr. Green's expert feedback about the emotional blockages that drive the cluttering behavior. She'll offer advice to others in similar situations or with similar emotional blockages, showing how to find relief and freedom.

Decluttering means slicing away the things that no longer serve you so that you can get the space, time, and positive feeling you need. This process is about creating and maintaining breathing room in your home and heart. It is a process that requires that we fully witness our complex humanity. Fully witnessing our lives in all their tangled beauty and trouble requires faith, insight, and diligence. It also requires courage, compassion, and patience. Fortunately, these spiritual energies already reside within every one of us.

We have perfect faith that you are already equipped to start this journey.

You've got this. Let's begin.

1

·····························

The Nature of Clutter

Bless your clutter.

Yes, you heard right: *Bless it.*

Bless everything in your life that is superfluous, broken, burdensome, and overwhelming—it is all here to teach you the most important lesson there is: what really matters. It will teach you about the importance of love, peace, and liberation—how to live authentically with only the things you really love and need. It is here to cast light on what is most essential to your health, happiness, and both human and Divine relationships.

Bless your clutter. It exists to help you discern what is truly important to you and what doesn't matter at all. It will teach you to distinguish between what is useful and meaningful and what has no meaning or purpose whatsoever.

In fact, decluttering is a deep spiritual practice that can bring you closer to your true self, the people you love, and your Divine Source. When you choose to declutter your life, you are embarking on a journey toward your Highest Self. The light that dwells within you will find room to stretch out and illuminate the path you walk. Your clutter is your guide to that open, light-infused place. Like crumbs left on a trail, your clutter is the road map that leads you—object by object, choice by choice—deeper into the life you want. With every piece of clutter you remove from your life—whether it is old newspapers, outdated clothing, worn-out relationships, self-defeating thought patterns, destructive emotional patterns, or spiritual blockages—you draw one step closer to the life you are truly meant to live. You deserve a life that is open, unburdened, joyful, and free.

You have the potential to create something beautiful in your life, inside and out. You have the power to choose. Realizing that you have this power is the beginning of your journey to a decluttered life.

So here's the deal, and it's pretty darned simple: Whether the clutter is in your home, heart, mind, or spirit; if it's weighing you down, crowding you out, blocking your light, cramping your style; if it's become an obstacle you keep stumbling over; if it continually cuts you with a broken, jagged edge; if it's stopping you from finding the things you really love, then it's time for you to *let it go*.

It's time for you to make some space for what truly matters. It's time you found a little breathing room.

The Nature of Breathing Room

Close your eyes for a moment and imagine yourself in a room that is empty yet remarkably inviting. This room is spacious and full of light. The window is open and a gentle breeze stirs the air. Morning sunlight is shining through the glass—a sweet, soft light. You are alone in this room, but you are not lonely; instead, you feel that the new day brings with it a lifetime of blessings. In your heart, you feel as open, fresh, and light-filled as the air. You feel the room reflecting your heart and your heart mirroring the room in an intimate and infinite reflection.

Even though the room has four solid walls, it feels expansive. Infinite. Whatever energy you invite in enters without obstruction: love, joy, compassion, courage, patience, kindness, strength. These energies become the air you breathe. They infuse you with life. Like breathing pure air, you know that only by releasing can you be filled up again. There is no struggle or clinging. Only ease.

This room is empty, yet you have no desire to fill it. Because it is already full. It is a space filled with pure possibility. This is your Breathing Room: the space you leave open and empty, for the sake of compassion, peace, love—for the sake of you. And it's time for you to move in.

Your Natural Resistance to Creating Breathing Room

In real life, it's not easy to create breathing room. It's the last thing we get to, if we get to it at all. And we will deny up and down and every which way that it's even possible to create breathing room in our lives. We can't imagine it happening. But that's the point: breathing room doesn't happen by accident, so if you are waiting for breathing room to appear on its own in your life, you will be waiting a very long time. *It needs you to create it and maintain it as sacred space.*

And therein lies the real challenge. We humans have a deep-seated need to fill empty spaces. We believe that the only things that are real are the ones we can lay our hands on. But what we fail to see is that empty spaces are full—full of pure potential, a vast openness into which we can invite any energy we desire. Because most of us are blind to the true character of emptiness, we are in a feverish rush to fill it. We think empty walls need more artwork. Empty spaces on our calendars need to be packed with activities. Silence needs to be filled with small talk.

We may temporarily create space in our homes and hearts, but we have a hard time holding that space. Our culture does not value emptiness. In fact, it generates fear and anxiety. We associate emptiness with loneliness, boredom, depression, economic scarcity—a lack of mental, emotional, and physical resources or options. We avoid emptiness because it frightens us.

Yet in the life of the spirit, emptiness is precious. It is the space into which we can breathe. It is the clarity into which intuition shines. It is what Zen Buddhists call "beginner's mind": a mind (and heart) free of the preconceptions that block wonder. If a child sees a butterfly flitting from flower to flower, she will run and flap her arms in an attempt to join the beautiful creature in flight. Her mind is not yet filled with the limiting idea that people can't fly. But adults can attain this mindset too: Orville and Wilbur Wright discarded that same notion and were the first humans to take flight.

Before you move any further down the road, it's important to remember that this is a process that requires gentle patience, coaxing, and compassionate self-awareness. Perhaps you are resisting decluttering, but you may sometimes feel that it is your clutter that is resisting you. Not everything wants to come loose immediately. What makes it difficult is the way your possessions are intricately interwoven with emotions, history, memory, and self-definition. When you attempt to remove physical clutter, it's important to be aware of this. Everyone declutters at a different rate. A desk drawer that would take one person ten minutes might take another several hours—or even several days. Only you will know what works best for you. Pay close attention to your own needs. Feel your deep emotions and share your significant stories. Listen to both with all your heart: it's the only way to sustain the energy required for your journey of liberation.

The True Nature of Your Heart

The heart is often a forgotten sacred space. The heart is meant to be touched by joy, laughter, happiness, and innocence. Instead, it often carries suffocating burdens: anxiety, fear, and worry. What is the heart's full potential? It can be a home where love abides with ease, forgiveness flows like fresh air, and gratitude is a constant, welcome guest.

In a world where stress, burnout, and breakdown are at an all-time high, many of us unknowingly block this sacred space. We do not treat our hearts with the care and tenderness they so richly deserve. Our hearts are uniquely beautiful creations meant to invite the Divine and reflect its sacred light. But instead, we treat them like dusty storehouses for our most painful emotions. We load up with regrets, guilt, fear, worry, and anxiety. We are unwilling to look at this emotional clutter, let alone sort through it and discard whatever is not useful or beautiful. We box up our troubles, stack them precariously, and then try to pretend they aren't there. Treating our hearts this way is like walking into a sanctuary and dumping an ashtray on the altar.

We can tell ourselves that it is only a temporary condition, that we will get to the work of unpacking our difficult emotions and take honest stock of them later, but in truth, the longer we allow them to sit, the more likely they are to get buried under other junk. We may have the gnawing sense that we have emotional stuff to take care of—but even this feeling gets buried in the piles of unwanted mess. Eventually you live by squeezing through the tight spaces of your heart, sidestepping obstacles on your spiritual path, and shutting doors to untended spaces.

It's no way to be. Your heart is a home for the Divine. It is your spiritual home. You live there full time. There are no vacations, relocations, or trading up for a newer model. So we have to learn to care for our hearts as our one true home.

You must find the compassion and the courage to face the tough emotions, pain, and patterns that keep your heart closed. You must take an honest inventory of the clutter inside you. Anaesthetizing yourself is not acceptable. You must forgive. You must meet the people in your life precisely where they are and yet be willing to leave them there to do their own work if they choose not to grow with you. Be open to change. Trust the process. Declare yourself worthy of the beautiful space you seek to inhabit. Creating space in your heart is by no means easy. But it's worth it. When you love and care for your heart in this way, your heart becomes a place where the sacred can dwell.

The True Nature of Your Home

When your home is open and inviting, it can be a sacred retreat of joy and light for you, and those you love. It can be a place where you find and offer forgiveness, where compassion is always present.

And like your heart, your home is a sacred temple where you can tap into your deep wisdom, commune with the Divine, and feel connected to your Source.

Yet, most of us underestimate the inherently sacred nature of our homes. We tend to treat our homes the way we treat our hearts: we burden them with unnecessary and potentially hazardous clutter. Stuff accumulates over the years because of our carelessness. Unaware of the energy that outdated and broken items project, we unknowingly dishonor the space that is intended to nourish us. A heart that is cluttered with worry, resentments, anger, guilt, and fear is a heart that will eventually become heavy, dark, and painful. A home that is cluttered with dusty and broken remnants of the past, unused and unloved objects, and heavy boxes that we are afraid to open is a home that will become difficult to live in.

One way to look at our home is purely in terms of functionality. It's a collection of rooms in which we eat, sleep, bathe, work, and hold conversations. Viewed this way, everything we do in our home is geared toward getting from one end of the day to the other. We launch ourselves through one activity just to make it to the next, never stopping to take stock of the miracle we are participating in. We wake up in our bedrooms groaning at the sound of our alarm clocks, then drowsily step to the bathroom for a morning shower, still grumbling. We get dressed—perhaps complaining that we can't find the clothes we need because there are too many items to sort through!

We then race to the kitchen to make breakfast (already running late, since it took so long to find matching socks). At the breakfast table, we shovel down breakfast while going over our plans for the day, then holler our farewells over our shoulders before rushing out the door to work. In this pattern, we don't offer gratitude for that first breath that draws us into consciousness. We shower without feeling thankful for the gift of warm, clean running water. We eat without savoring our food, speak without thinking, and hear without listening. After a while, we forget that we live in a sacred space, where eating is a beautiful ritual of nourishing the body, sleeping is a gift of rejuvenation, and waking is a blessing beyond measure. Rather than looking at our houses and the lives they support as vivid, unique, compelling, and miraculous, we see them as wholly unremarkable.

But nothing could be further from the truth. Your home is the sacred heart of your unique, divinely created life. When you begin to live intentionally, you'll be less likely to clutter your space with extraneous stuff, actions, and words. Instead, you'll add to the rich fullness of your life. You will be able to identify and repair the ways you unconsciously neglect your space. You can live more thoughtfully, gratefully, gracefully, and peacefully.

The Nature of Your Emotional Clutter

You've heard the expressions before: Consumed by fear. Consumed by resentment. Consumed by worry. Consumed by guilt. Anxiety. Despair. Disappointment. Bitterness. Envy. Why do we call these feelings "consuming emotions"? It is because they draw an enormous amount of energy from us, but they give us nothing valuable in return.

To be fair, these emotions are trying to help, in their own way. Indeed, they want to prevent pain. Take resentment, for example. Resentment exists to prevent you from re-experiencing harm; it is trying to protect you from the people who have hurt you in the past. Resentment takes up space in your heart, like an angry gatekeeper pounding his fist into his hand, waiting for a hostile interloper to attempt entry. It's the same with other consuming emotions: they exist to shield us.

But these kinds of consuming emotions do not just block pain; they also become the clutter that blocks our hearts. We keep them around because we think they will be useful to us. We are afraid to let go of them—on some level, we feel we are going to be in trouble without them. So we stash our resentments, just in case someone wants to harm us in the future. We collect our worries, in case we need to be reminded of what might go wrong. We hoard our guilt in the event we need to remember the time that we could have been a better and more upstanding person. Our anxieties gather like dust and become so thick we can barely see through them.

With all of this junk lying around in the sacred space of your heart, how can light and air move through? The space is devoured by our consuming emotions, robbing us of time and energy. We can try to push all of this away to the dark recesses of our hearts and deny that they are there, but we will begin to feel heavy and burdened; our vast inventory of consuming emotions will make it impossible to enjoy the vibrant and beautiful space that is available.

Consuming emotions and the gratitude for life's blessings simply cannot share space together. Ask yourself: Have you ever gnawed on a bitter resentment while enjoying the sweet air of spring? Have you ever held tightly to righteous anger while noticing the simple beauty of a rose? Of course you haven't. Heart clutter makes it impossible to see the miracle of life that is blossoming around you. The world wants to move you to love. It wants to inspire you to action. It wants to motivate you to truly live the life you are meant to live—but it has no way in because of all the darned junk.

As we get deeper into this book, we'll discuss how to release the emotions that are holding you back from the life you want and

deserve. But that process starts with your physical clutter and recognizing how your consuming emotions drive you to consume the
goods that consume the space in your home.

The Connection Between Consuming Emotions and Consumer Habits

In the same way that heart clutter makes it impossible for you to
enjoy your amazing life, your physical clutter makes it impossible
to stretch out and enjoy life in your physical home. Our consumer
habits perfectly mirror the habits of our hearts. We fill our homes
with the kind of clutter that we carry inside—things that we tell
ourselves may be useful down the line, but which end up making it
impossible to enjoy anything. Ironically, we often bring the clutter
into our homes to quiet our consuming emotions.

We buy timesaving devices because worry tells us that we are
running out of time. We purchase carloads of objects we don't need
because we envy the lifestyles of people we imagine are happier
than us. We load ourselves down with needless trinkets because we
are driven by the anxiety of scarcity—or because bitterness insists
we are entitled to material compensation for our emotional woes.
Our lives are overburdened by physical reflections of our emotional
exhaustion.

In the end, the things we buy to simplify our lives end up com-
plicating them. Gadgets and gifts that are supposed to bring us
happiness and freedom actually suck happiness and freedom out
of our lives. Think of all the "time-saving" devices you may have
collected over the years. The things that were meant to save you seconds, minutes even: choppers, blenders, infusers, removers, stackers,
and holders—these things consume your time because you have to

move them to find what you actually need. These things are not only consuming physical space and time, but they are also taking up mental and emotional energy. Like their emotional cohorts, they make it impossible for you to truly enjoy your home.

How much time, energy, and space are you surrendering to the things that are consuming space in your heart and your home? You don't have room for them. You don't have time for them. Here's the honest truth: *you only have room and time for what you truly love.* When you choose that over clutter, you nourish your physical health, emotional growth, and spiritual expansion.

The Path to Your Breathing Room

Remember that room you imagined before? The beautiful, light-filled space with the breeze? Right now, close your eyes and visualize yourself standing in the center of that room. In your mind's eye, stretch your arms out wide. Open your fingers. Spin your body around. Feel the empty, free space around you. You move without fear of bumping up against anything that could hurt or entangle you. Breathe the fresh air deeply and smile. See the golden light streaming in. Let its color reach into you and touch your heart. Everywhere you look in this room, there are reminders of beauty, miracles, happiness, and love.

Now, open your eyes and see the room you are physically sitting in right now. Perhaps your heart sinks a little because the room you are in looks *nothing* like the room in your mind. It might seem overwhelming in comparison.

The answer is easier than you ever imagined: you begin right where you are. The path between the room you are standing in and the room you want is directly under your feet.

All paths to liberation begin with the chains of suffering. The path to peace begins with unrest. The path to wisdom begins with unknowing. If we want to get to where we are going, we must first compassionately accept where we are—then take one brave step forward. We cannot relinquish our burdens until we are able to release the very first thing. Our acceptance of ourselves is the open door that leads us toward liberation.

Compassion

Once we feel determined to change, we want to throw ourselves into the task with a fierceness that reflects our determination. We see a pile of clutter and want to attack it. We throw ourselves into a task with all the energy we can muster, and we attempt to lay waste to the enemy. Remember those consuming emotions we talked about? If we use the same emotions that created the clutter to try to clear the clutter, we will ultimately defeat ourselves. Sure, it may be a great initial burst of energy (nothing like a good dose of pure fury to get things moving, right?), but in the end this pace is not sustainable. Chances are, you will burn out quickly and be left in a pile of emotional and physical rubble.

And even if you *were* to make it all the way through your clutter to that beautiful, wide-open space you imagined, you will arrive in a state of rage and self-affliction. Not quite the grand entrance you want.

You are not battling clutter; you are relieving yourself of it. You are releasing it. Compassion slices through clutter the way insight cuts through illusion. With compassion, as with insight, suddenly that which seems complex becomes simple. That which was murky becomes clear.

It is not always easy to have compassion for the things that cause you pain and discomfort. You might have trouble mustering compassion for the dust-gathering objects that make it impossible for you to appreciate your home; for the difficult feelings that clutter your heart; for relationships that are a source of anguish. It can feel especially challenging to feel compassion when it feels as if these very things are making your spiritual life a virtual impossibility.

However, compassion is precisely the prescription for all these problems. At some point, everything you have taken into your life, your home, your heart, and your spirit are things that held a promise of happiness, freedom, joy, ease, or love. We need to acknowledge that everything that clutters our homes and hearts originated with such a promise. The clutter's lifespan must end when it no longer offers you what it promised. So, it's time to thank our clutter compassionately and let it move on when it has:

- lived out its promise of happiness, freedom, and so forth for a time but is no longer able to fulfill it
- seemed to have created happiness or freedom for other people (even just the people in advertisements or commercials) but never did anything for you
- never had a chance of fulfilling its promise to you

So, if something, someone, or some feeling makes a promise of help to you that is simply not what you want or need, you can smile and say: "Thanks, but no thanks. You are not bringing me happiness, and I have to let you go. I am grateful, but I have to send you on your way."

We misunderstand what it means to have compassion. We think it means welcoming whatever life brings without discernment or

exception, accepting all things equally. We believe that having compassion means never hurting anyone's feelings. We think that having
compassion means never saying no. But does having compassion
mean holding the same space in your home for your wedding album
that you do for the dishwasher manual you haven't touched for seven
years? Does it mean giving the same amount of time to your child
and the unannounced neighbor who drops by to gossip? Does it
mean entertaining every worry that passes through your mind? The
truth is that having compassion means that you must sometimes say
no to the things that drain you, so that you can offer an unequivocal
and resounding yes to the things that feed you.

Decluttering is an act of compassion—for yourself and for others,
because it frees you from draining influences so you can give yourself over fully to what you love and care for.

Decluttering is looking at the dishwasher manual and saying,
"Thanks for making yourself available to me for the last seven years,
but it looks as if I don't really need you. I have limited space. I am
sorry, you just don't make the cut."

Decluttering is telling the neighbor who comes over to gossip, "I
appreciate you dropping by, but I promised to spend time with my
child."

Decluttering is telling the worry that pops into your head,
"Hello, worry. I know you showed up because you have something
you want to tell me. But I just don't have room for you. I don't have
the time to entertain you. And I certainly don't need to give you a
permanent residence in my sacred home."

By releasing the clutter in your life—whether these are cluttering
objects, conversations, relationships, or emotions—you are saying to
each, "There is a place for you, but not in my home, my heart, or my
life. Your path does not cross the threshold of my inner sanctum."

Allowing clutter to linger is not an option. It is dishonoring a space that is Divinely created and inhabited. Hesitating about what to release is not an option, because indecision is not compassionate to yourself or to the other. You must be decisive. You must take action. In order to find the breathing room in your life that you need physically, mentally, emotionally, and spiritually, you must compassionately SLICE through your clutter.

The Essential Need for Safe Yet Permeable Boundaries

All homes, regardless of size, shape, or location, have some essential elements in common. There are walls that keep its inhabitants safe from unwelcome intruders, a roof that protects from the elements, doors for people to come and go through, and windows that allow light and air to flow in.

A house that is too open will be overrun by pests, thieves, and all manner of unwanted elements. A house that is too open is unsafe for its inhabitants. On the other hand, a house that is too closed-off will also suffer from a lack of safety.

A healthy home must have permeable borders. It can be neither too open nor too closed. It must have doors and windows that open and close to allow in people, objects, light, and air. And what's more, you must be the person who decides what comes in and what goes out. You are the gatekeeper of your home. You decide what constitutes an emotionally and physically healthy, decluttered home. Whether we are talking about people, objects, or elements, you must be the one to decide what comes in and what stays out. You must decide what visits and when it should leave; what takes up permanent residence, and what never crosses the threshold.

Your heart should have the same flexible boundaries. It should be capable of opening and allowing in honored and beloved guests, but not be so open that people who bear ill will can come in and steal what's most precious to you. On dark days of the soul, you can welcome others into your heart so they can find shelter in your warmth. But you have the right to request respect, kindness, and gratitude, even in the midst of trouble. If there are people in your life who simply cannot understand this—who prove time and again that they are unwilling or incapable of offering you these essential gifts—you must find enough courage and fortitude to bar the door and let them know they are unwelcome. Folks who are motivated to return will change. If they truly value you and the gifts your heart offers, they will come back humbled and willing to be good, respectful guests. People who can't or won't treat you with respect and gratitude may act wounded when you turn them away. (No one *but no one* likes being broken up with.) But believe me, they will find somewhere else to go. They will find some other home to trash, another heart to take advantage of.

Having boundaries does not mean cutting yourself off from the world. It does not mean disallowing either joy or pain. It means creating a strong container, through which your own boundless, spiritual light can flow and through which spiritual nourishment can return to you. With strong boundaries, you become a beacon of light and strength that others are drawn to for warmth and safety.

Being a Role Model for Self-Respect

Another important reason for having good boundaries around your home and your heart is that it sets the tone for respect. People earn the respect of their peers and their community by showing integrity: living in accordance with their values.

A house whose sacred nature is disrespected from inside won't earn respect from outside its doors, either. Clutter, mud, and dust will accumulate; precious treasures will be lost; and no one will see this as anything other than the status quo. To put it simply: no one will honor your home if you do not.

But if see your home as sacred, you will fill it with things you love that honor your home's nature and bring you a sense of meaning and well-being. If someone tries to sell you something that doesn't fall into those categories, tell them you're not buying. Whatever they are offering is not going to increase the sacredness of your home. If someone were to come into your home and leave their stuff lying around, you could clearly see that it doesn't belong. This is the clear benefit of having respect for your home, and ultimately, others will respect your boundaries when you are absolutely clear on what they are.

A heart can suffer from a similar lack of self-respect. A heart which does not know its own sacred nature or its values does not have a system to identify intruders. It will be overrun by energies that seek to erode its beauty, clarity, and peace. A heart littered with disappointments, resentments, indignation, hateful notions, and inflated worries will certainly attract more of the same. What's another grudge, on top of a lifetime of grudges? What difference does another anxious thought make when your mind is already swirling with them?

If you have people in your life who try to stir up these emotions in you (let's admit it, we all have people in our lives who are thrilled to dump their negativity on us), you will not be able to fend them off unless you have good boundaries and respect for the sacred nature of your own heart. You do this the same way you protect your home. If someone comes to you peddling the junk of worries, anxiety, gossip, doubt, and cynicism, you can send them away before they've finished making their pitch. Let them know you are sure there are plenty of people who would welcome those things, but that brand of clutter does not go with your décor. And frankly, it never will.

By respecting the heart of your home and the home within your heart, you encourage others to respect you. This kind of respect is contagious. When someone tries to breach your boundaries, an alarm will go off. Such intruders will have a new awareness. They will notice the way you shake your head yet smile compassionately. They will realize that they have something sacred at stake too. Your behavior will remind them that they have the ability to feel self-respect; they can insist on respect from others, just as you do.

Know your boundaries. Feel strong and assured in protecting them. They are not only a gift to you—they are a gift to every person you encounter. By caring for the sacred nature of your heart and home and maintaining boundaries that allow life to flow safely in and out of your home and heart, you are showing the world what sacred looks like. You're saying: *This is how sacred happens.*

STEP ONE

stop and
listen

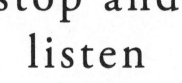

2

....

Stop

Here's the thing about clutterers: We like to talk. Specifically, we like to talk about our clutter. We like to talk about clutter like two old curmudgeons sitting on a park bench, who would rather gab for half the day about their ailments than spend half an hour at the doctor's office getting cured. We like to talk about how badly we're cluttered. We like to talk about how we're swamped in clutter.

Many of us have developed an amazing sense of humor about our cluttering habits. We laugh about clutter. We joke about clutter. We could gab about clutter for ages. And why not talk about it? If we can't do anything about it (and many of us have tried, without long-term success), we might as well develop a vocabulary, story, or shtick around it that makes it understandable. Relatable. Even laughable.

When I was interviewing people for this book, I started with a simple phone conversation to explore the emotional sources of the

cluttering behavior: spiritual blockages. Everyone found these conversations enlightening. There were some genuine ah-ha moments.
At the end of each phone conversation, I made an appointment to go
to the client's home.

On the appointed day, I showed up and knocked on the door.
The client welcomed me, and might offer a warm hug along with an
apology for the state of their home.

In the kitchen, we once again took up the topic of their cluttered
home. I would ask some questions about how they were feeling,
scribble a few notes, and take a sip of tea from the mug graciously
offered to me. Then I would ask: "So, where should we get started?"

And then there would be a stunned silence as they stared—like
they no longer recognized me. After a moment, they blinked. Their
eyes would begin to dart around their home as if looking for the
closest trapdoor. "You mean you actually want to do this?" they
asked incredulously.

This question came up so frequently I simply had to shake my
head and smile. "Talking about clutter doesn't clear the clutter any
more than talking about meditation could bring about enlightenment,"
I said. "If you want the benefit, you actually have to do the work."

To be fair, all that nervous chatter about clutter makes sense. It's
a natural, evasive defense. Let's face it—clutter makes us nervous. It
starts our minds spinning. We think, "How in the world did it get
this way?" and "What kind of a person lives like this?" and "I'll bet
I'm the only person I know with something to hide." Our nervous
chatter, both internal and external, can send us running in emotional circles of self-judgment. Our messages to ourselves send us
pinging between guilt and regret and fear and worry.

The first thing we need to do is to stop chattering about our clutter and let our clutter speak to us.

So the first step in SLICE is simply: STOP.

Stop where you are. Don't run. Your heart rate may rise. Your breathing may get shallow. Your feet may start twitching and your hands may start shaking. Your eyes may start shifting around, looking for the most expedient escape. But know this: *You are not in danger.* Your clutter is not going to kill you. It is not a threat to you. It will not undo you. As you stand your ground, you are what you always have been, spiritually speaking: You are whole. Complete. You are stronger, wiser, and more courageous than you believe.

The feelings we have about our clutter are deeply uncomfortable, if not painful. Your emotions may feel downright dangerous, threatening, or menacing. And what do we do when we are in pain, or feeling uncomfortable or threatened? We do what's most natural: we run.

It's natural to want to escape from physical danger or pain. When we are truly hurt or threatened, it is in our best interest to pay attention to those signals. Interestingly, we have the same response to mental and emotional pain and discomfort as we do physical pain—it can be hard to distinguish between them when your senses are heightened by fear. When you are looking at your clutter, you may want to do anything to get away from it. Your body will tell you it is a threat to your safety, integrity, or well-being.

However: your clutter is not a tiger in the wild. It will not devour you. In fact what it is, *is* you. The clutter is an outward manifestation of your internal life. That's probably not a feeling or idea you want to shout from the rooftops. But that's okay. We create our clutter unconsciously, through indecision, fear, and running away. And that's okay too. You've done what you've done and you are where you are. Stop and accept it. This can be undone and you are the one person who is empowered to undo it.

Stop in this moment and experience your new awareness of the fear and indecision you've been unconscious of for so long. Remind yourself that what has built over time can be undone through your inborn decisiveness and courage. With mindful awareness, you can master your impulse to run.

Why is that impulse so strong? We all have the vestige of our early animal brains. It is geared to protect us from danger. Sometimes this part of the brain gets triggered into a hypervigilant state. It's very powerful—it really believes your clutter is a tiger. At times, the fearful feelings it produces can control us. But there is another part—one which modern neuroscience indicates is the most highly evolved area of our brain. It's the part of our brain that is responsible for compassion.

With compassion, we take the next step in the SLICE method: LISTEN.

3

Listen

Take a deep breath. This may be difficult if your animal brain has gone into hyperdrive, but think of it this way: your animal brain is like a frightened stray in need of love and nourishment. Though it may bare its teeth, it mostly wants you to back off so that it can escape. But escape is not in its best interest, is it? Rather than escape, your animal brain will benefit most by being welcomed. It needs your loving and compassionate presence. You are the one who can care for it, and listen to the plaintive cry beneath the fearsome growl. You are the one who can calm it, befriend it, and ultimately transform it.

So listen to your clutter. *Yes, clutter speaks.* It speaks volumes! It can tell us about our attachments, fears, and worries. It can regale us with regrets about missed opportunities or our disappointments in life. This is not easy stuff that our clutter has to say. Facing our clutter is nothing less than facing the neglected parts of ourselves. We have to be willing to silence our judgment (of ourselves and our situations) and simply accept where we are in the moment.

Listen to your feelings about your clutter. It's okay. What is it that you are feeling? Guilt? Shame? Overwhelm? Confusion? Anger? Blame? Worry? It's okay. Keep listening intently. Breathe into your feelings with compassion. This is just your fearful animal brain baring its teeth. These feelings aren't going to kill you. They are seeking acknowledgment. Listen, but don't let them back you down. Pushing them away will do no good. Instead, talk to them with understanding and compassion, with the intention of easing and transforming the pain.

We must begin by acknowledging these emotions, but we can't stop there. If we do, they will not loosen their grip on us or our clutter. Each of these emotions, in its strange and backward way, wants the best for you—but they're trying to get their point across by bullying you. No one can be forced into being their best self. If anything, emotional bullying and coercion only results in us shrinking from our highest potential. Once we acknowledge these bullying emotions, we must learn how to transform them.

Let's take a close look at these emotional bullies, the negative feelings you associate with your clutter. Just like the child on the playground who twists your arm for lunch money because his stomach is twisting with hunger, every bully is hurting inside. They want attention and power, but they are too emotionally stunted to ask appropriately for what they want. Looking into the wounded heart of bullies can transform them and turn them into allies and possibly even friends. But we must be willing to stand firm and listen. By staying present with the consuming emotions that we carry in our hearts, we can understand them, answer them, and make them our allies in the decluttering process.

Guilt

Listen to Guilt. Guilt tells us that we are less of a human being than we ought to be. It says we should have done better in life and dealt with this mess long ago. We should have taken the time to make our home an inviting place—but we didn't. And now it is an unmanageable mess. It's all because we are less than we ought to be. We are alone, lonely, and frightened, and we deserve to suffer. A better person—a more organized person, a more courageous person—wouldn't be in this position.

Answer Guilt. To Guilt's oppressive harangue you must answer patiently, "I understand that you want me to be a better person. You are suffering because you are comparing me to some fictitious perfect human being and finding me less than adequate. But listen to me, Guilt. It's okay. I've made mistakes in the past. But I am no less than any other human being—and there is no such thing as a perfect person. I simply am who I am. I've been where I've been." Fear of being judged as less than perfect has brought us to this point. But you don't need to be afraid anymore.

Transform Guilt to Support. Once you acknowledge that Guilt's fear of imperfection is based on illusion, you can loosen its oppressive grip on you. Guilt can then become its better self: Support. Guilt might have told you, "A good mother would never throw out any of her child's artwork." Support will now say, "How can I help you sort through your daughter's artwork, keeping the most important drawings and recycling the ones that neither of you really remember? Let's invite your daughter to help—this will be fun. You are a great mother to have kept these for so long. Now, let's work together to make this a joy for both you and her."

Shame

Listen to Shame. Shame is telling you: "I need to go hide somewhere where no one can see who I truly am. I am abhorrent. If I were a good person, I wouldn't be in this state. I am responsible for where I am and for what I have become. I am sick. I am ugly. I am beyond help. Get away from me so you won't be contaminated by my presence. Walk away and leave me alone. It's better for both of us."

Answer Shame. To Shame you must say, "I am not going to turn away. To me you are not abhorrent. You are beautiful. Life has been unkind to you. It has scraped you up and left behind a mess. I see that. But you are not a mess. You are made of love. You are meant for love. And I am here to love you. Come closer, so I can see all of you. There is nothing to hide here. There is only light and healing and warmth."

Transform Shame to Openness. Shame is a fearful response to a world that is hurtful. It wants you to stay small. It wants you to hide so the world can't see the fullness of you. It is afraid that if you do show yourself to the world, you risk being wounded. Once you understand that Shame is a form of protection, you can encourage it toward growth and change. What Shame really wants is for you to survive; what it doesn't understand is that life is about more than surviving. It is about thriving, which only happens when we expose ourselves fully. Shame's timid protectiveness can be transformed into Openness and a willingness to grow.

Overwhelm

Listen to Overwhelm. Overwhelm is saying, "This is too much for me. I am too small. I am too weak. You are asking too much of me. I can barely hold myself up on my weak little legs. You want me to do more than I am capable of doing. I have taken on one burden after another, and though each on its own may seem small, their cumulative effect is crushing. You are asking me to accept your kindness, but I fear that if I accept one more thing, I might collapse under the weight."

Answer Overwhelm. To Overwhelm you must sweetly insist, "I am not asking you to take on any more. In fact, I am offering to lighten your load. I see that life has asked you to carry so much—and you have piled your own expectations on top of it. Part of that burden is your own unfair idea that you must handle all of this on your own. It is a weight that you cannot continue to carry. Here, let me help you. Let me take that expectation away. I am here for you."

Transform Overwhelm to Mindfulness. Overwhelm just wants the world to slow down. It has a hard time breaking down processes into component parts. On its own, Overwhelm is incapable of sorting through objects, information, or feelings. It sees everything as a tangle of inextricable and confounding knots. Overwhelm is always on the verge of panic, and the harder it tries to extricate itself from these knots, the tighter and more impossible they become. It needs you to breathe. To smile. To know that this is not a race. There are no deadlines. Overwhelm wants to see into the knots and untangle them.

With your calm and steady presence, its burden can be relieved. It will be transformed to Mindfulness.

Confusion and Indecision

Listen to Confusion and Indecision. These twin emotions are trying to tell you: "I cannot begin to sort through what is important and what is not important. Life is asking me to think too quickly. To judge without truly seeing. To choose without truly feeling. I once thought I knew what mattered. But I don't know any longer. Everyone has different values. My parents. My faith. My peers. My professional colleagues. The media. Everyone is shouting at me to come in their direction. I don't know which way to turn, so my only option is to stay put just where I am."

Answer Confusion and Indecision. You must reason with Confusion and Indecision. Say, "You want to move forward, I know, but you are terrified of making a mistake. You think: What if you move in the wrong direction? What if you listen to the wrong voice? What if you have to cope with regret? Everyone is exhorting you to choose what they feel is most important. These voices make a cacophonous jumble in your mind. All you want to do is just hunker down and cover your ears. But listen: there is one very quiet but important voice that you are not yet hearing. It is your own intuition. Come with me, dear one—away from the noise and chaos. Come to the quiet place where you can hear the whisper of your inner voice. It knows just what to do."

Transform Confusion and Indecision to Gratitude and Discernment. Confusion and Indecision perceive value in everything.

Confusion feels so grateful for everything that it can't seem to make sense of anything. Indecision hangs on to all the possibilities that Confusion lays at its feet and can't decide what stays and what goes. They can't seem to see the varying gradations of importance in the pile of clutter. So we must transform Confusion into Gratitude by acknowledging our appreciation for all that we have. Then, we use Discernment to divide the things that we feel grateful for that have a place in our homes and our hearts, from the ones we release with thanks. With your newfound understanding of these twin emotions, you will be able to use Gratitude to truly appreciate all you have been given and Discernment to release what needs to move on.

Anger and Blame

Listen to Anger and Blame. They bare their teeth and growl: "This mess is all your fault! Look what you've done! Anger is all I have left—my last refuge. I may be alone, but by God, I am powerful. I see the fear in your eyes: it gives me energy! You are completely incapable of managing your life, and now I have to pick up the pieces. It's unfair. Why should I have to deal with all your crap? I'm the victim. People say they care but they are liars and frauds. The only energy I can rely on to get me through life is my own fury. Now get out of my way!"

Answer Anger and Blame. Look Anger and Blame in the eyes—and smile. It is the only way to disarm them. Whisper: "I see that you feel stranded. I see that you are exhausted. I know that the energy you draw from is a dry well. You are thirsty. Follow me to the stream that flows from the river of forgiveness. You will be refreshed and gather your strength—but it will be *true* strength, not energy drawn from the last vestiges of your adrenaline. You need rest. You have been awake for too long, waiting for the next attack on your well-being. I am truly sorry for what you have been through, but what you are doing now is only going to draw more of the same trouble. We can change this together."

Transform Anger and Blame to Strength and Acceptance. Anger and Blame are naturally protective. They are furious, righteous energies that want to show how strong and powerful they are. But the energy you need to sustain your decluttering efforts requires you to be calm and rested. Once you have listened to Anger and diffused its adrenaline-laced energy—washed it in the cooling waters of forgiveness—you will be able to feel your true power. You will understand that your true Strength is derived from your willingness to forgive. From this Strength comes Acceptance of where you are in this moment. There is no more running. Once you have transformed Anger and Blame into Strength and Acceptance, there is no need to run.

Worry

Listen to Worry. Poor Worry. Worry wonders where its next meal is coming from. Worry fears that no matter how much nourishment is offered, it will be the last bite. Worry cannot rest or trust. It looks to the future and sees nothing but impending disaster. Worry always prepares for the very worst, believing that if it does not look out for itself, disasters will surely happen.

Answer Worry. With Worry, it is important to be firm. "Look, Worry," you must say. "You have feared being alone and you are alone. You have feared you are in danger and you are now in danger. You have feared the world is loveless, and you live in a world without love. Everything you have feared, you have manifested. You will always live with the thing you fear most. You fear the cruel, cold judgment of the world, and now you live in a cold and cruel world of your own creation where you have appointed yourself the judge—and no other judge is quite as harsh as you. Listen, Worry. You are only harming yourself. Love is trying to find you. Faith is trying to warm you. Joy is trying to touch you, but it cannot reach the dark corner you are crouched in. You must trust that nothing you fear is quite so terrible as the reality you have created for yourself."

Transform Worry to Faith: Worry is afraid that everything is going to go wrong, which means that deep down Worry believes it is possible that everything can eventually be right. Your ability to maintain hope despite Worry's steady stream of what-ifs will help you to turn it into Faith. Every worst-case scenario can be transformed by a faithful stance. Worry wants to know: "What if everyone finds out about my clutter and stops respecting me?" You can say, "Everyone has clutter. Acknowledging it openly will make me more connected and supported." Faith can change Worry's perspective. Faith can meet everything that might go wrong, every anxiety. Turn over your worries and let go of your fears.

By listening to Guilt, Shame, Overwhelm, Confusion, Indecision, Anger, Blame, and Worry, we have transformed them. They have now become Support, Openness, Mindfulness, Gratitude, Discernment, Strength, Acceptance, and Faith. These new emotions are the emotional and spiritual tools you will need for the important work of decluttering your home, heart, and life. Just by listening, you give yourself what you need to begin your journey.

So now what? Do we go in and start throwing things away, willy-nilly? Move as quickly as we can, tossing everything in sight?

No. Anything done without purpose or a clear intention is eventually going to circle back around and create more problems. Before you remove a single thing, you must take the next step in the SLICE method and *Intend*.

STEP TWO

intend

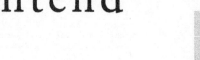

4

....

Intend

In order for us to declutter spiritually, we must set an intention for the space we are working in, whether we are talking about a whole room, a drawer, a closet, or a piece of furniture. Beautiful, clear spaces begin with intention.

Think for a moment of a beautiful resort or getaway—one with those gorgeous patios that are open to ocean breezes, where sunlight gently cleanses everything. It's the kind of place where someone can truly relax, unwind, and completely let go. Did the people who designed those spaces design them without intention? Of course not. A hotel without intention is not going to draw anyone; at its worst, it might attract people who are having such a bad life experience that they don't care what kind of cluttered environment they are sitting in, so long as they have a place to throw their own stuff.

No, those five-star resorts are designed with impeccable intention. Those companies know what kind of experience you are looking for: happiness, peace, relaxation, and rejuvenation. And so they begin with that intention. You must do the same with the spaces in your home. You must set an intention so that positive energy can manifest. You must be clear about what you want; then, when what you *don't* want shows up in that space, you can see it is clearly out of place.

Chaos may happen accidentally, but peace manifests by intention. Fear and anger may bubble up without warning, but courage and kindness grow through intention. Anything positive we want in our lives begins with intention. Beauty also arrives in our lives unbidden, like a special grace—but without the power of our intention, it will quickly disappear, covered in uninvited clutter.

So we must ask ourselves the questions: What do I want this room to do for the people who are in it? What do I want it to do for me? How do I want to feel when I am in this room?

Some of you may not feel you are entitled to make such a bold, self-determined decision. You may have never really asked yourself, "How do I want to feel in my home?" You bought your home or signed the lease, moved in, and brought all your physical and emotional clutter with you. Everything about your past and your feelings about it just followed you in and landed where it pleased. You have allowed everything to pile up without a second thought or consideration of what energies you wanted to invite into your life.

Well, this is your chance to start over. Imagine, envision, and question what you want. What energies do you want to invite into your home? What feelings do you want in your heart?

To your emotions, you are a wise, compassionate presence. You were able to look at the difficult feelings, truly listen to their needs, and answer them with compassion. You have transformed them into powerful allies. You speak their language. Now it's time to figure out what feelings you *do* want.

Do you want your living room filled with joy? Say it, and by golly, say it boldly and proudly. Do you want a bedroom that is a peaceful, restful haven? Own it! Do you want a kitchen that percolates and bubbles with health, creativity, and laughter? That's awesome. Sing it out—and mean it. You really and truly deserve the energies you intend.

✳   🏠   ♥

Decluttering the Past and Making Room for the Present Moment: Hope's Story

Hope and Jon have a bedroom.

Technically speaking, that is. They have a room in their home with a bed in it.

Unfortunately, it isn't a bed that either of them sleeps in regularly—and they rarely sleep in it together. These days, they both avoid the bedroom like the plague. At the days' end, Jon usually falls asleep exhausted on the couch with the TV droning an electronic lullaby, while Hope retreats to their guest room, the only room kept open and free of clutter.

It's no wonder that the bedroom is a space that the two of them avoid. Hope and Jon's bedroom is not a relaxing place to hang out. It is not a place to unwind from the stresses of daily life, not a place to relax or to surrender from wakefulness into sweet dreams. Playful pillow talk or meaningful discussions don't happen here, much less emotional or physical intimacy.

It wasn't always this way for Hope and Jon. They met nearly twenty years ago and their love developed around a shared sense of humor. Hope remembers a time when their life together felt fun and filled with adventure; they were best friends and coconspirators. They used to hang out for hours, laughing and talking. Their bedroom was a place where they would have deep discussions or share funny stories. It was a place where they could relax in one another's company and simply feel grateful that the universe brought them together.

However, the last few years have been hard for Hope and Jon. The turn in the economy resulted in Hope losing her job. Though she was able to find part-time work, her underemployment has limited their cash flow, putting a financial strain on their married life. Not long after losing her job, Hope's brother died of acute alcoholism. Hope gained weight and she no longer feels attractive or fun. In the wake of all this devastating loss, their bedroom has become a burial ground for grief, disappointments, unfulfilled dreams, buried anxieties, and misplaced fears.

Though it is decidedly a small room—with just enough space for a bed, two end tables, and a large chest of drawers—there is a cramped and airless feeling in the room that comes from more than just its size. It feels almost as if any joy that had ever been in the room has been squeezed out.

Going through Hope and Jon's room is like performing an archaeological dig through their years of difficulty, loss, and deprivation. There is a palpable emotional heaviness in it. This heaviness is embodied by a cumbersome chest of drawers (ironically painted a brilliant electric blue against the muted browns of the bedding and the walls). "I hate it," says Hope. "As soon as I clean it out I want to take an axe to it!"

The blue behemoth sits awkwardly in the corner of the room, blocking access to their shared closet. As Hope begins to sift through the clutter in her room, she first comes across a layer of trash sitting out on the top of the dresser. The familiar stuff of daily life: receipts, wrappers, rubber bands, and other discarded items, including a handful of Jon's cigarette butts. "Trash is trash," says Hope. "It's easily identifiable and I know what to do with it." It didn't seem like such a hard job—at least at first.

But she doesn't have to dig very far before she comes across items that are not so easy to part with. Not everything is what you'd expect. Some seem so inconsequential that you'd wonder why in the world Hope would hesitate to toss them, like the receipts and the rubber bands.

She finds, for example, a PEZ dispenser in one of the drawers of the hulking electric blue dresser. "Even though I can't tell you when or where I got that PEZ dispenser, I'm reluctant to toss it. Telling you about it now it sounds silly, but I do know the thought that went through my mind: *The PEZ dispenser represents quirkiness, youth, and a sense of fun. If I throw it away, I feel as if I am saying that I am no longer cool, fun, or any of the positive feelings I associate with the toy.*"

It turns out that the blue dresser is a repository for memories of happier times. Hope pulls out two his-and-hers college t-shirts that have definitely seen better days. "We never wear these. I mean, we finished college twenty years ago. But when I look at them I think of how happy life was back then. How carefree and easy. Part of me really wishes life could still be like that. I feel like if I give up these t-shirts, I give up any hope of ever being that happy again."

Not everything in Hope and Jon's room represents their relationship with one another. Some of it represents Hope's unkind judgments of herself. On the night table next to Hope's side of the bed are three books, all about diet. The book on the top of the stack prominently features the word *FAT* in bold, bright letters on its dust jacket. The book is literally dust-covered. When asked how she feels when she looks at that stack of books, Hope looks defeated. "I feel terrible about myself. It reminds me that I have gained weight and that I have not been able to lose it. I also have some jeans in my closet from when I was skinnier, but at this point, when I look at those jeans, I just feel like I haven't been able to achieve my goals."

A gift bag is also on the night table—very pretty and delicate, covered with colorful paisleys and golden glitter, but empty. When I ask where the empty gift bag came from and why it is in such a special spot, Hope explains that the bag was from a gift exchange at her former workplace. "It was our annual Christmas party. It was so much fun and I just remember having such a great time and everyone smiling and laughing and hugging. We were all so close. I've told myself that I kept the bag because it's pretty. Well, it is. But there are a thousand bags just like it in the store. And if it was really about wanting to use it to give gifts, I suppose I would have given it away already. I mean, it's been three years. I think I am keeping it because it reminds me of how great things were at my work. And I think I'm still finding it hard to believe that it ended so quickly and so completely."

Sitting on the corner of her bed, Hope looks down at her hands. "There is one more thing," she says quietly, with tears glistening in her eyes. "In the corner of the closet, there is a bag with a set of pajamas. They belonged to my brother. I can still smell his scent on them. The way he smelled before things went bad. His hair gel, mixed with the soap he used. I never really got to say goodbye. The last time I saw him, I was in such a rush to get away."

She pauses and takes a deep breath. Dust motes play in the sunlight streaming through the windows.

"I'm afraid that if I get rid of his things, he will disappear from my life completely. Like he never existed. What if I forget him?"

Dr. Green Weighs In on Hope's Clutter

It's very clear that Hope and Jon are living in their past. Their bedroom has become a sort of tomb in which they have buried their love under piles of disappointment and grief. They are afraid of vulnerability—of exposing their love to the light and the fresh air of the present moment. Instead, they live in a perpetual state of nostalgia, hoping that the happiness they experienced in the past will sustain them and their love.

But the past contains both joy and pain. Unfortunately, Hope and Jon's unwillingness to sort through their emotions and face them with courage and compassion has created an unbearable stew of emotions. Both their happiness and grief were unexamined, so everything has become stagnant and stuck. It is all tucked away, hidden, and covered up by a dusty layer of anxiety.

I think about Hope's chest of drawers as a metaphor for her emotional life. She just sticks things in there that she doesn't have the energy to sort through or face up to, telling herself, "I'll deal with that later." Then she shuts the drawer and puts it out of her mind.

But not really. Out of sight is not out of mind—not at all. In fact, every time Hope puts another object in that piece of furniture, it becomes heavier, literally and emotionally. And when she looks at that chest of drawers (painted a color that cannot be ignored, by the way!), she knows in her heart that there is painful stuff in there. Even her happy memories do not really inspire a sense of happiness in the present, but a remorse that the current moment is not happy. So the happy stuff actually creates depression instead of happy feelings.

It is impossible for Hope and Jon to be intimate in their bedroom, much less let themselves feel vulnerable. They are in a constant state of vigilance. They are guarding against their own unhappiness. They never know what remnant of the past they might stumble over or what emotional injury they might end up reopening. They cannot relax in that room because they are literally living with ghosts from the past.

Real, vital, and robust happiness can only be created and experienced in the present moment. In order to do this, the two of them must sort honestly through the past and be willing to release it and bless it. They can express gratitude for their early courtship, college days, things they once laughed at—then, with that blessing, let those experiences flow outward into the world to become a blessing to others and the universe.

They have to be willing to fully experience grief and let their emotions touch them deeply. Hope has not completely experienced her sadness, remorse, or grief because she is afraid of going through the transformation that will happen on the other side. The truth is, we can all be made new through our difficult emotions. We have no need to fear the process. For example, a butterfly becomes strong as she struggles to make her way out of her cocoon; this strength enables her to take flight. If she were to try to live in the cocoon in a suspended state, she would perish. If we tried to preempt her struggle by cutting her out of it, she would never gain the strength to stretch her wings.

So we must have the courage to touch every object in our rooms, listen to the stories they want to tell us, and allow our emotional reactions to flow all the way through us. We must have absolute trust in the process, so that we may stretch our wings out in the sun and take flight on love's fresh air.

There is a paradise waiting to be born within Hope and Jon's bedroom, in their marriage, in their life together. I have hope for Hope. *And for you.*

Lauren Helps Hope Declutter Her Bedroom

Hope runs her hand absently over her thin tan bedspread as she scans the clutter in her bedroom. She shakes her head and turns her attention back to the bedspread. "Once I get this room cleaned up I'm going to invest in something nice for this bed. A really pretty, warm comforter set. Once I'm done decluttering, I think I'll have earned it."

I smile at Hope. "What makes you feel like you don't deserve it now?"

She looks back at me with an eyebrow raised. "Shouldn't I set a goal and reward myself when I am done?"

"I think you are worthy of something beautiful and warm to wrap yourself in right now. When I look around this room, I see a person who does not believe she is worthy of something special. Something beautiful. I don't think you need to earn beauty and warmth, Hope. I think you deserve it. You don't have to be more or different or better. You are enough. Right now. And you always have been."

I smile at Hope as she wipes away a tear.

"When I look around your bedroom," I continue, "I don't see anything that's reflective of the energy of love, of warmth, or of intimacy. I want you to get yourself that comforter set, something really beautiful that you can imagine yourself and Jon wrapping up in at night. Snuggling under. I want you to be able to imagine the two of you laughing together. Not about the past, but about the day you are in. The moment you are in. Taking delight in one another—and again, not a memory of who you were twenty years ago, but who you are now. Embracing one another just as you are— not young college graduates but interesting people in the center of their remarkable lives.

"Once you find that comforter, put it on your bed. It will shift the energy in this room. It will become the anchor in this room, which will say to you, 'This room is not a storehouse for difficult memories. *It's a love den.*' I smile knowingly at Hope and she smiles back.

I advise that she use the comforter as a symbol to guide the process of deciding what stays and what goes. The comforter becomes a symbol of love, warmth, intimacy, and happiness within the present moment. As Hope picks up items and makes decisions about them, she is to ask herself, "Does this object go with my comforter? Is this object a reflection of the light of love that beams in this moment?" If the object is a reflection of that light, then it will stay. If not, I tell Hope to move it into another room or a storage space where it actually belongs or get rid of it altogether: goodbye dust-covered diet books!

Hope nods her head and beams. She gets it. Then her countenance changes, as if she remembers something that is troubling her. "What about my brother's things?"

I sit in silence for a few moments. "You loved your brother very much. But you have attached yourself to his memory—you have not really let him go. I have an idea."

"I'd like to hear it," she answers.

I tell her that perhaps she could write a letter to her brother and tell him what she needs to say: how much she loved him, how hard it was to watch him self-destruct, and how much she misses him. Then she can take her letter with his clothing and commit them both to the earth.

Hope closes her eyes and takes a deep breath. I wait quietly for her to share. "My mother never let us have a memorial ceremony for him. It was too hard for her."

"You need that closure," I tell her. "I want you to purchase a flowering tree and plant it over the clothing and the letter. Let the sun shine on it. Let the rain water it. Let the air touch it. Allow your memory, all your grief, and your brother's life to transform into something beautiful and new. You don't have to lock his memory away in a dark corner or hide it in your closet. You can let it touch the light of day. You can help it move on in an appropriate way. You can transform it."

Setting Your Intentions

What energy do you want to create in each space in your home? What energy do you want to *thrive* in there? As you declutter, you will stay true to the intentions you set. For each room, we have given you some words to use as prompts. We suggest you begin with just three or four words, so the intention is easy to remember. Stay absolutely focused on the intention as you declutter. You may choose from the words we've provided or you can decide upon your own.

Whatever you choose, we suggest that you make a sign to hang in the room as you declutter that says, "This room was made for _____." We have provided a template for you to download and print. Visit www.beyondword.com/product/breathing-room and look under the Free Media section. Many of our clients choose to keep these signs hanging in their rooms: when clutter begins to creep back in, they can remember to stay powerfully and courageously connected to their intention.

5

....

Your Home Entry:
Room for Open Invitation

*The moment you are willing to change, it is remarkable how the
Universe begins to help you. It brings you what you need.*

—LOUISE HAY

It's nighttime in the dead of winter. A chilling wind whips around
you as you fumble in your coat pocket for your keys. Looking up, you
see a light shining in the doorway and you smile. That doorway sig-
nifies so many positive associations for you: safety, rest, comfort,
belonging. Placing the key in the lock, you turn the knob. You are
home, surrounded by familiar sights. You enter the front hall, a place
of transition. It is the place where your inner world meets your outer
world. This place always offers you the first warm embrace of home.
It is where you leave your belongings, unwrap yourself, and unburden yourself. When you leave, it is where you make your preparations
to move into the outside world. Here, you hug your guests hello and
goodbye. You thank the person who delivers packages. You kiss your
children and wish them a great day.

Our home entries may look different. For some, they are grand entries with soaring ceilings; for others, a narrow hallway with a small coat closet—or perhaps no more than a small area rug marking the entry of a one-room efficiency apartment. Some entries contain a small table where we toss our mail. Others are littered with colorful children's backpacks, boots, and scarves. Some people may share their entries with housemates and roommates. They all have one thing in common: they are the introduction to the home. The place that says, Welcome. This is where I live.

What do you want to invite into your life? Life is flowing with energies that are yours for the taking—love, happiness, kindness, courage, and creativity. Setting an intention for your home entry is a perfect opportunity to answer this deeply important question.

The physical entry to our homes, like the spiritual entry of our hearts, needs to be an open, inviting, light-filled space. Who do you want to invite into this sacred space? What do these people represent to you? What energies do you want to invite into your heart? How can you make both of these spaces—the home within and the home without—open and free? Choosing the intention will allow you to feel happy, brave, and confident about opening the door wide and sharing the bounty of your life within.

The Spiritual Importance of Your Home Entry

Life is full of trouble and difficulty. We have all experienced it. We all know the truth of what Buddha taught: in life, everyone experiences pain. This is part of what it means to be alive; there is no avoiding it. We will suffer. We will experience loss. This all sounds very profound, and perhaps profoundly depressing. But it's not. Buddha taught something else too—everything in life is impermanent. It comes and it goes. This is true of pain and happiness.

But if we bar the doors to our homes and our hearts, ostensibly guarding against the difficulty that will come or the happiness that may leave, three things happen. First, the pain that comes in cannot get back out. Second, the happiness that we guard so carefully will become stale and eventually expire. And third, no new happiness can find its way in. We need to find a way to keep the channel clear, so that our emotions do not become stagnant.

Decluttering your life all begins in the entry to your home and heart. It begins when you clearly state what you want to invite into your home and into your life. Do you want happiness? Love? Ease? Supportive friendships? Strong and loving family relationships? Abundant success? These are all wonderful intentions.

We want you to think of all of these things as honored guests. Whatever it is you want in your life, they need room to move in. They need room to *move*. Most of all, you need to step out of the way and allow it. You have to believe you deserve all those things you want. And that means that you have to move the clutter that is blocking it.

A heart that is welcoming draws positive energy to it. It attracts good people, good vibes, and good fortune. Perhaps you know people like this, whose hearts are so open and warm that people gather around them like a hearth, for warmth and comfort.

Similarly, a home that is welcoming also draws positive energy. People enjoy being there. They feel whole and welcome—like they can stretch out and be themselves. They can express themselves fully. They feel they can unwind.

Decluttering your entry, whether it is a grand foyer or a simple hallway, sets the stage for the life you want to unfold within. Just as your heart must speak its truth in order to invite what it needs to thrive, the entry to your home needs to declare what it wants. That way, your home can be the beautiful, vibrant place it is intended to be.

Possible Intention Words for Your Home Entry

Open. Inviting. Warm. Kind. Loving. Joyful. Life-giving. Accepting. Embracing. Uplifting. Friendly. Welcoming. Affirming. Hospitable. Relaxing. Peaceful. Happy. Supportive.

A Blessing for Your Home Entry

May the entry of my home be filled with the light of kindness and the warmth of welcome. May its doorway serve as a healthy boundary between my self and the world outside. May it allow in people and energies that serve my highest purpose in the world, and act as a barrier to anything that would harm me or drain me of my precious energy. May it be blessed with countless warm embraces and joyous reunions. May its walls reverberate with laughter and shouts of joy. May all who are allowed entry find peace and solace within; may everyone who leaves learn that they have grown in heart and in spirit.

An Exercise for Decluttering Your Home Entry

Walk into the doorway of your home as if you were a guest, visiting for the first time. Stand outside your door and call to mind three words of intention representing the energy you want to manifest there. Imagine opening the door and having that energy flow out toward you, touch your heart, and lift it up.

Now open your door and walk into your home. What is the first thing you see? What is the first thing you feel? What might block that light from touching your heart? Remove the first thing that feels like an energy obstruction. If this thing does not belong in your house, remove it altogether. Put it outside to donate or carry it to the trash. If it belongs somewhere else in the house, take it to the area it was intended for.

Go outside again and repeat the process: intend, envision, enter. Are you feeling uplifted now? If not, look for another source of your "blocked" feeling and remove whatever's triggering it.

Repeat this process until you have cleared the energy. Remember you are entering each time with fresh eyes. Once you have established the right energy, you may move objects into the space that resonate with that energy. If you intend freshness, perhaps fresh flowers. If you intend cheer or joy, a bright vase or painting. If you intend strength, a solid sculpture of stone or wood. If you intend wisdom, a framed painting or photograph of a wise being.

First impressions make a difference, and you should feel as welcome and loved in your own home as any visitor. You are, in essence, test-driving your own welcoming experience. Whatever you find in the entry of your home, you are saying, "This is what you can expect to find within."

6

....

Your Living Room:
Room for Relaxation
and Happiness

*Now and then it's good to pause in our pursuit of happiness
and just be happy.*

—GUILLAUME APOLLINAIRE

Stretching out on the couch at the end of the day, you feel like you can finally be yourself—no more expectations, no more to-dos. You take a deep breath and allow yourself to sink in. Maybe you are surrounded by friends who've dropped by to watch a basketball game on TV, your coffee table loaded with chips, salsa, and drinks. Or perhaps your children are stretched out on the carpet playing a game of Monopoly while you attempt to read a novel. Maybe you thought you had the couch and the remote control to yourself, until your partner comes in, takes the remote from your hand, turns off the TV, and asks you to make room so she can snuggle in next to you. Or maybe you are simply enjoying the quiet solitude you've longed for all day.

Living rooms are places we share ideas, stories, excitement, and affection. They can also be places where we entertain guests. They can be a retreat where we go to unwind alone after a hard day's work.

Some homes have a dedicated living room, while others have more than one. Still others might find this place to unwind is their front porch. If you live in a small apartment, you may entertain guests on a futon that converts into a couch. Wherever you unwind on your own or with friends and family, wherever you welcome others to sit down and relax—that's your living room.

We all long for the experience of unwinding and enjoying life. We work for it. We toil for it. Would it surprise you if we told you that we also seem to avoid relaxation like the plague? Have a look around your living room, the room that has been set aside for the simple pleasure of relaxation and joy. What do you see?

Televisions. Computers. Piles of unread magazines and books. Homework. Bills. Looking around our living rooms, we see reminders of why we *can't* unwind, why we *can't* relax. And how can we, really, when our living rooms remind us that we are always just one unpaid bill, one disturbing news story, one infuriating blog post, one urgent email, one uncomfortable phone call, or one thankless task away from the joy and the relaxation that eternally await us?

The clutter in our living rooms prevents us from experiencing the feelings it was created for. The same can be said of our hearts: if we truly wish to experience the joy and relaxation that is our honest birthright, then we have to overcome the habitual thought: *if we can just push through, relaxation and joy will be our reward.*

The Spiritual Importance of Your Living Room

We seek happiness; we struggle to find it, but ultimately we cannot be happy until we realize that happiness is not something to be found at the end of striving. It is not an object to be grasped at, but an energy to allow. On our path to happiness, we bypass happiness. So rather than chasing what we desire, perhaps it is best to stop and invite it to come to us, through us.

Happiness and contentment, two of the energies we hope to realize in the space of the living room, are like companions who come to us when we relax. Have you ever had the experience of getting quiet—stopping the chatter in your head—and suddenly being able to hear the birds singing? It's not that the birds weren't singing before; it's that you were too distracted to hear them. When we are conscious, awake, and in gratitude, we find that happiness comes to us unbidden, like the sounds of birds singing.

There is a space in our hearts like the living room, a favorite place where we sink in when our work is done. Where we can slowly look around and realize that everything we need to be happy is there. Our lives are filled to brimming with blessings. There is beauty around us, soft light, smiling faces of loved ones, joyous music, and laughter. Are you aware that all of this exists in the living room within?

You don't actually have to be done with your daily work to sit in the living room in your heart. Just take a moment and imagine that you are about to leave for vacation—you have tied up all your loose ends. Go home to the living room in your heart and relax in complete contentment. All the noises of life's business are turned off. As you envision this, repeat this mantra to yourself:

My work is done. There is nothing more to do.
Smile.

And how wonderful to know that we can invite others into this space as well, to share our happiness, blessings, to life stories—to share life itself.

This is the purpose of having a living room in the home and the heart—to relax, take stock of blessings, invite happiness, and share life itself. If you find that your living room (either the one in your home or the one in your heart) is not serving this purpose, it is time to remove the clutter that is getting in the way of this rich, deep, joyful experience.

Releasing Old Knowledge and Making Room for Your Wisdom: Joel's Story

Ten years ago, Joel and his wife, Shelley, moved into a house that they share with Shelley's ninety-two-year-old mother. They were faced with a dilemma: Joel was being forced into retirement because the company he was working for downsized. For most people, that might be unbearable, but for Shelley and Joel, it was simply a challenge. They tried to find the silver lining in their difficult situation. Their willingness to find the good in every situation is simply their spiritual habit: Shelley and Joel are some of the most optimistic people you will ever meet. Their faces are always glowing with warm smiles, and they are quick to wrap you in a genuinely affectionate hug. When Joel was let go from his company, he did not spend much time fretting or worrying. He took it as an opportunity to learn and to grow. He began to collect books about meaningful retirement. He is a naturally curious man with a great love of learning. He is also naturally gregarious and sees it as his role in life to reach out and make an impact on the lives of others. He and Shelley share this quality.

When I come to help declutter their home, they are happy to show me around their home. We spend some time talking about the principles of spiritual decluttering—they catch on quickly. It's important to note here that not all decluttering clients are created equal. Some people will agree with everything I say *in theory*, but they don't trust the process. They will fight tooth and nail over every sticky-note pad, unmatched sock, and outdated magazine. Not so with Shelley and Joel. I explain the fundamentals: how it's important only to keep items that have significance attached to them. They immediately begin to make a pile of art objects and travel memorabilia that they like, but don't love.

This is too easy, I think. Everyone has something they have trouble getting rid of. For some people, it's clothes. For others, it's children's toys, artwork, or dishes.

We are working in their shared office space when Shelley looks at her watch. "Oops, I have to go take my mom to her doctor's appointment."

She gives Joel a kiss on the cheek and he smiles like a schoolboy in love. She gives me a hug and as she draws me close, she whispers in my ear, "Maybe you can talk to him about his books."

Ah . . . that's it: books.

Joel is a smart man who has never stopped learning. This is part of what makes his retirement so vital, interesting, and meaningful. But once he has learned something from a book, the book stays put. Joel treasures knowledge. But his books are becoming burdensome clutter.

Dr. Green Weighs In on Joel's Books

Books represent more to us than just abstract knowledge and stories. They are, in a sense, autobiographical. Books represent turning points in our lives: moments that we came alive, had an awakening, or realized something about ourselves or the world. Moments when we realized that we were not crazy, not alone. We think: there are people who agree with me. Other people have taken my experience and represented it in poetry, stories, and with historical or scientific evidence. Books tell us, "You are real. You matter. You exist!"

One of the hoarders I worked with on the TV show saved tons of books. When I asked him why, he told me, with tears in his eyes, "When I didn't have anyone, books were my only friends."

When you pick up a book you can go into an alternative reality. You can move away from your pain and feel comfortable. Books make you feel whole in a world that otherwise feels broken. Books can help us make sense of a seemingly nonsensical world. In this way, books are medicinal.

However, when do you stop needing the medicine? When it is it time to pass the medicine on to someone else? At some point, our books can become crutches: we can stand on our own, but we don't trust it. We feel like we need something to lean on or we'll fall. And we really do need to pass that particular medicine on—not just because another person could use it, but as an affirmation that we don't need it. We need to release the crutch so we can see for ourselves that we have the strength to stand on our own. We have to trust that we have actually internalized what the book has to teach. We are living proof of its knowledge. We have to let our books go so that they can work their magic and their medicine in the world.

Lauren Helps Joel Declutter His Books

We are crouching down next to a low bookshelf, examining a particular set of books: the ones that Joel purchased when he was let go from his job. At that time, Joel, in his ever-optimistic way, decided that he would not only retire meaningfully, he would teach others to do the same. So he purchased every book he could find on the subject of meaningful retirement. He pored over the books and absorbed everything they had to share. When he and Shelley relocated to their new home, he offered a course on the subject to other retirees—those who had chosen retirement and those who were pushed into it. His course taught retirees that this was not the end of the road, the end of life's adventures, or the end of learning. It was just the beginning.

This was ten years ago. Joel hasn't picked up the reference books since.

"Joel, may I propose something to you?" I ask.

"Of course," he says, smiling.

"I don't think you need these books anymore."

Joel raises an eyebrow.

"I don't think you need these books because I think you know everything in them. In fact I think you know *more*."

Joel smiles.

"For the last ten years," I continue, "you have been living the message of meaningful retirement. You are walking, talking empirical proof that it is possible. You could probably write a book that is better than any of these."

Joel smiles broadly. "You're right. I could probably do a TED talk about it."

"Could and *should*," I affirm.

Joel picks up the books and walks them over to the giveaway pile. He steps back and looks at them, crossing his arms over his chest and nodding.

"That feels better," he says.

Affirming your own wisdom always does.

Possible Intention Words for
Your Living Room

Relaxing. Shared. Fair. Soothing. Enjoyable. Understanding. Energetic. Friendly. Dependable. Comfortable. Comforting. Easy. Happy. Fun. Involving. Magnetic. Accepting. Warm. Listening. Informed. Inspiring.

A Blessing for Your Living Room

May I abide in peace in this place and find rest here. May my eyes be open to my many blessings: life, family, and friendship. Remind me that this space itself is a gift of comfort, free from fear, distraction, and worry. May happiness arrive as a most honored and beloved guest. May I find the peace in this space and in that peace, may I grow the capacity for happiness. May we share joy here, and may this room always retain some measure of our joy, providing light and comfort in times of distress. May this living room be a room filled with the breath of Life: a Living Room and Living Refuge.

An Exercise for Decluttering Your Living Room

If this room is made for relaxing and enjoying blessings, then we must remove the clutter that is obscuring those blessings from being seen. This is the definition of a decluttered home, heart, and life: one where blessings are in clear view.

Take out a camera (or use the camera on your phone) and take a photo of the blessings you see in the room. Reviewing those photos, are you able to see those blessings clearly? Or are they blocked? Are grocery store flyers sitting on top of your treasured books? Is there a hoodie tossed over your grandmother's photograph? Are there newspapers with stories of traumas covering up the clay pinch pots your child made at camp?

Sometimes when we just scan a room, it's easy to overlook our blessings (as well as what is hiding them). This exercise allows you to take stock of how many blessings and inlets to happiness there are in this room—as well as a clear visual record of what's blocking them. Once you have reviewed your photographs, go back and remove the blockages. Then, stand back and take a photo of the whole room.

When you've completed the exercise, tune in to your intentions. Does the room resonate with them? If not, go back and repeat the process, hunting for the things that obstruct your blessings. When the room is fully unblocked and you can sense that your intentions are fulfilled, sit down and relax. Your work is done. There is nothing left to do but invite happiness in.

7

....

Your Dining Room:
Room for Nourishment
and Sharing

*Sometimes you struggle so hard to feed your family one way,
you forget to feed them the other way, with spiritual nourishment.
Everybody needs that.*

—JAMES BROWN

Your dining furniture could be a simple card table with mismatched chairs, an ornate antique mahogany table with chairs to match, or a couple of bar stools pulled up to a kitchen counter. A dining room is more than just a room in which you eat. It is a symphony of sensation. It's a place where stories are shared, silverware clinks against plates, steam rises from dishes passed graciously from hand to hand, and voices rise in loving crescendo. We appreciate one another in the dining room. It's the place where we nourish our bodies and our souls—and that is just when we are eating!

Dining rooms can double as computer areas, conference centers, homework stations, and art studios. These days, dining rooms are multitasking marvels, centers for family functions and personal projects. The life of a dining room can be rich and complex. Which sometimes means that it can be the most cluttered room in the house. It's not that we should never use our dining rooms for multiple tasks. But we need to be intentional about how and when we use our dining rooms, so our multitasking does not interfere with our appreciation and understanding.

How rare is it that we sit down with those we love, in gratitude for sharing the bounty of life giving nourishment? Rather than being a wide-open space adorned with fresh flowers and laid with delicious, nutritious meals, our dining room tables are more likely to be makeshift desks or multitasking workstations. They are staging centers for feeding frenzies and indigestion, where food disappears without ever being appreciated or tasted; where real conversations are dispensed with as we stuff ourselves before we run off to the next activity. Even when we sit with those we love, we often ruminate in our own worlds, rather than make heartfelt connections.

Our hearts, like our bodies, are meant to be nourished: with love, gratitude, and mutual enjoyment. The clutter in our dining rooms prevents us from truly tasting and experiencing the food that nourishes our bodies, partaking in conversations that feed our hearts, and appreciating the relationships that feed our souls.

The Spiritual Importance of Your Dining Room

What makes a meal memorable? The best meals are a feast for the soul; they nourish us completely. They touch every part of our being: physical, mental, emotional, and spiritual. They make us feel connected to one another, to our history, to the earth that feeds us, and the Source of the earth's bounty.

But most meals aren't like that at all. It's a straightforward trans-action: we're hungry, so we eat. We need calories, so we put them in our bodies. Heck, we don't even need to *taste* the food to get the calories, so we don't bother slowing down or enjoying it. A computer is good enough company. A television is good enough company. A car is good enough company. Or so we think.

We spend a significant amount of time thinking about food. We spend little time savoring it. So the question is: what gets in the way when it is time to sit down and enjoy a meal?

Would you be surprised if we told you it was clutter? Yep. Clut-ter. Anything that keeps you from experiencing the sustenance and the love we share at the table is clutter.

Should we work at the dining room table when we are eating? Nope. Homework or study at the table when a meal is being served? Not a good idea. Smartphones? Sorry. (You don't already spend enough time on your smartphone? Come on.) Headphones at the table at mealtime? No way. Contentious conversations that make it difficult to taste your food or digest it well? Better saved for another time and venue.

We could focus on two simple things: food and people. Very straightforward. We could simply experience gratitude for two elemental blessings: nourishment and good company. Instead, we plop the distractions down right in front of us, deliberately blocking out the world. Why are we shoveling food down so fast that we can barely taste it? Why are we rushing to clear our places? What is the "better" thing that we are trying to get to?

We all live under the illusion that real satisfaction is somewhere off in the future. So we rush through our meals. We rush to swallow each bite of food, preparing for the next bite before we've even had a chance to taste what's in our mouths. We believe the next bite is more delicious than the one we are chewing. If we could truly declutter our dining rooms, we could really focus on the nourishment, sustenance, and love that is present at that table. Then, perhaps we could experience that nourishment deeply and come to see that the sustenance is sitting in front of us and love is right beside us. There is no place to run to when what we seek is right here, right now.

Possible Intention Words for Your Dining Room

Nourishing. Fun. Quiet. Conversational. Sharing. Shared. Enjoyment. Laughter. Savoring. Healing. Togetherness. Kindness. Ease. Joy. Vibrancy. Health. Wholeness. Friendship. Relationship.

A Blessing for Your Dining Room

May all who sit down at this table be thoroughly nourished: body, mind, heart, and spirit. May their needs be met. May what they consume nourish their deepest needs and help them grow in strength and vitality, so that their lives may be of service. Let not the poisons of hatred, fear, and anger be served at this table. May we be warmed by what we consume. May each of us leave this table feeling that we have partaken in the miracles of food, family, and friendship. May we never take these things for granted, for the awareness of the miracle of nourishment is perhaps the greatest blessing of all. May we receive the strength to return to this table to be blessed yet again.

An Exercise for Decluttering Your Dining Room

In our work with individuals and families who are cluttered, we find that the dining room table is the most multipurpose piece of furniture in the house. It's a homework station and a bill-paying center. It's where kids come to play games. Adults come to craft and piece together their artwork. And all of this is wonderful—until it prevents you from using your dining room table for its primary purpose: to provide physical and spiritual nourishment to the people who break bread there.

This exercise is one that helps you turn your multipurpose table into a single-use table.

Make a list of all the things you and your family do at your dining room table: homework, office work, crafting, corresponding, games, sorting mail, and so forth. You are going to create a container for each thing on the list. Even though none of these activities may technically be clutter, it definitely becomes clutter during a meal—and it might prevent you from using your table at all. Have your boxes ready. When it is time to eat, you are going to put the office work in the office box, the crafting supplies in the craft box, the toys in the toy box, and so on. Then, you are going to remove the boxes from the dining area while you eat.

Why remove them? Remember that anything that prevents you from absorbing blessings into your system is clutter. When we eat, our bodies absorb nutrition through our intestines and send those nutrients out into the bloodstream to the parts of our bodies that need them. But this is not the only way we absorb nourishment. We absorb beauty through our eyes and flavors on our tongues. We absorb the music of laughter through our ears, and we absorb love through our hearts. All of this requires focus. In Lauren's family, after the blessing for the food is recited and everyone says amen, someone at the table rings a small meditation bell. While the bell is ringing, everyone takes three mindful breaths to truly let the blessing of the meal, the company, and the love that is shared at the table sink in.

Single tasking at mealtime allows us to truly absorb all the nourishment our meals have to offer. Single tasking gives us the chance to savor the tastes and digest our food. It allows us to participate in rich conversations, laugh with a whole heart, and to truly soak in the blessings of those who are sharing the meal with us. Single tasking at mealtimes is a practice in being mindful of the gifts of food, family, and friendship. When dinner is done, everyone is smiling, and the table is clear, your table can get back to its multitasking life. You can return to your multitasking as well and you will do so with a full belly and a full heart, mindful of the blessings of both.

8

···

Your Kitchen:
Room for Collaboration
and Creativity

*In order to create there must be a dynamic force,
and what force is more potent than love?*

—IGOR STRAVINSKY

Our kitchens are natural gathering places. At parties, before mealtimes, while pouring coffee, or steeping tea, friends and family members lean against counters with cups, glasses, or plates in hand and simply feel at ease. If someone is cooking a meal, she might invite someone she loves to come join her in the kitchen. The conversation takes on the fast-paced rhythm of chopping vegetables or the slow, languid rhythm of a wooden spoon stirring a simmering pot of soup. Kitchens feel private, intimate, familiar. Perhaps it is because our nourishment comes from them—we feel fed simply by being in them.

Our kitchens store the rudiments of our sustenance, to be sure—pots and pans, staples of our meals—but they also store the ingredients for elaborate creative plans: exotic ingredients, high-tech cooking instruments, cookbooks with mouthwatering pictures. They also hold our ancestry: our grandmothers' pie pans, family recipes that are so familiar that they no longer need to be measured, ingredients for folk remedies.

Kitchens are where we create and connect. Here, it is easy to feel connected to our essential loving self, creative passion, and ancestral roots. It's easy to see why many people feel that their kitchen is the heart of their home. It also makes sense that when our kitchens are cluttered, our hearts can feel blocked or undernourished.

"What's for dinner?" It's a question that can exhaust us or enliven us, drain us or fill us with inspiration. And it depends on a couple of things: What do we have stored in our cabinets and fridges? Who are we collaborating with? And who are we cooking for?

If our cabinets are bare—or if they are filled with junk foods that are full of fat, additives, and empty calories—the thought of creating something new can be uninspiring or even demoralizing. If the ingredients are stale, mushy, tasteless, and dry, then we have no hope of making something we're excited to serve.

Food is not the only clutter we might be harboring in our kitchens. Many of us hang on to pots and pans, plastic storage containers, spatulas, strainers, and all manner of handy-dandy mixers, juicers, slicers, blenders, and choppers (not to mention all those twist ties, rubber bands, and plastic bags). If we are honest, we probably realize that we only use a small portion of these tools. Of those three cookie sheets you keep under the oven, you know you only use the one that sits on top.

If we have either food clutter or cooking device clutter in our kitchens, we might find that our kitchens have become uncomfortable places to create. We all have a hard time letting go of things we know to be inherently useful or which have value because they were given to us by someone we dearly love. At the same time, your kitchen isn't as useful as it could be if your counters and cabinets make it difficult to find what you need or cook what you want.

We have storage cabinets of sorts in our hearts as well, places where we store thoughts, ideas, feelings, impressions, and spiritual truths. Depending on what we store in our hearts, we can be inspired or we can stand with our hands on our hips, wondering what to do next, while our souls grumble in hunger.

The Spiritual Importance of Your Kitchen

Do you know that wonderful tongue-in-cheek Peggy Lee classic "Is That All There Is?" Between refrains of the song, Ms. Lee, in a voice dripping with boredom, tells one tale after another of how she had hoped for so much in life, but in the end, time and again, she got nothing but disappointment. At the end of each verse, she asks, "Is—that—all—there—is?"

We're willing to bet that you have wandered into your kitchen many times, hoping to find something delicious, savory, and soul-stirring, and then opened up the pantry or the fridge and wondered to yourself, "Is—that—all—there—is?"

We may very well have all the ingredients we need to stir up the deeply nourishing, soul-stirring feast that we long for, but we can't muster the energy, the enthusiasm, or the creativity to make it happen. So we go for the easy stuff: the junk, the quick fix. We grab super sweet, excessively salty, horrendously fatty, I-know-it's-bad-for-me-but-just can't-help-myself snacks that leave us hungering for more of the same.

If we allow our kitchens to be consumed by clutter and we always head for the quick fix, we are missing the wonderful opportunity to bring together nutritious, life-giving ingredients in ways that satisfy the body and the spirit. Cooking is an essential creative act that—at its very best—is an expression of love and care, for oneself and for others. When we cook, we are bringing to life the axiom that "the whole is better than the sum of its parts."

When we cook, we create something much greater than the ingredients could possibly be separately, and in doing so, we nourish people with the beauty and the flavor of their union.

Possible Intention Words for Your Kitchen

Creative. Collaborative. Nourishing. Colorful. Vibrant. Open. Clear. Healthy. Courageous. Inviting. Appreciative. Grateful. Delightful. Engaging. Fulfilling. Enriching. Supportive. Inspirational. Satisfying. Loving.

A Blessing for Your Kitchen

May this kitchen be a source of nourishment. May the meals created here be of service to the Divine One who created the food it contains. May we cook and eat with mindfulness and awareness. May we see the miracle of sustenance and life within every morsel of food and not eat with greed. May the cabinets be filled with enough food to meet the needs of this household, but not so much that it goes to waste. May we remember that not every being walks this planet with a full belly or a full heart, so let us be grateful for our abundance. We pray that all beings be relieved from the suffering of physical, emotional, and spiritual hunger. May the food I cook in this kitchen strengthen me to bring about a day where no more hunger is felt, when all may sit down in peace and find their bellies filled with food and their hearts filled with love.

An Exercise for Decluttering Your Kitchen

Take out your comfort food. All of it. The stuff you go to for your quick energy fixes and your emotional eating jags. Lay it all out on the counter. We want you to have a conversation with it. Seriously. You might think it's silly, but this will be helpful in the long run. We promise.

When we reach for comfort food, it's for powerful reasons. We are usually:

- exhausted
- anxious
- nervous
- depressed
- insecure
- fearful
- distracted
- numb

Recognize some of those feelings from our previous discussions? Yep, those are the consuming emotions. We consume comfort food when we are feeling consumed ourselves. We seek external comfort when we don't have the patience, strength, or awareness to find comfort within. So talk to your comfort foods and tell them why you go to them. Then, tell them what you are going to do the next time you feel the need for comfort: something truly and deeply comforting. Your conversation may go something like this:

"Potato chips, I usually run to you when I feel anxious. But the next time I find myself looking for you, I am going to take three deep breaths instead. If I am truly hungry, I am going to go for a bag of carrots."

Or:

"Strawberry licorice, I eat you when I am exhausted. But the next time I find myself hunting for you in the back of the cabinet, I am going to lie down and listen to my favorite music instead. If I'm truly hungry, I'm going to grab an apple."

We are not telling you to throw out every bit of junk or comfort food. Everything in moderation, right? But there's a connection. The consuming clutter in your heart drives you to clutter your kitchen with food that doesn't feed your soul. If you are sad or angry or fearful, then your heart is in need of true nourishment that these things can't provide. And if you don't step out of the negative feedback loop, you are just piling clutter on top of clutter, moving you in the opposite direction from holistic health and spiritual vitality.

Now that you've decluttered the food that is blocking your health and spiritual vitality, you are going to remove the cooking tools that are blocking your creative vitality. These implements clutter your drawers, cabinets, and counters, making it virtually impossible for you to move freely around your kitchen. They may very well be preventing you from using the space as you'd really like to. We want you to go to your favorite cookbooks and plan a meal that is a delight for the senses. Go wild. Plan every course. Imagine the party you will throw and the delighted faces of your guests as you serve up this amazing multi-course meal: hors d'oeuvres, soup, salad, main dish, side dishes, dessert, coffee, tea. You name it. This is your fantasy meal.

Now that you have your meal planned, go through the menu course by course and pull out everything that you would need to make that meal: pots, pans, bowls, blenders, and spatulas. Get all of it out on the counter. Now stop for a minute. If this is all you need to create the *best* meal you could possibly make—a meal to delight palates, hearts, and souls—do you really need much more than this?

Now we'd like you to declutter anything you have in your kitchen that is a duplicate of any of those things you've placed on the counter, which includes less useful versions of the same tool. So, for example, if you put a mixer on the counter and you have another mixer that just doesn't work as well (and you clearly do not have a need for two mixers to make this fabulous meal), then it is time to let go of the lesser mixer. This goes the same for salad servers, steamers, frying pans—all of it. The point is, if you don't need it to make the most fabulous meal ever, why *do* you need it?

You can repeat this process several times with different imaginary menus. If there is cooking gear that never makes it out onto the counter for any of the fabulous meals you imagine, remove it for donation or the dump.

One last thing: Go ahead and cook that fabulous meal, for real. Invite your family and your friends to enjoy the food you prepare in your healthy, joyful, creative paradise. You've decluttered your kitchen. You have something to celebrate!

9

Your Child's Room: Room for Growth and Change

Your children are not your children. They are the sons and daughters of Life's longing for itself. They come through you but not from you, and though they are with you, yet they belong not to you.

—Kahlil Gibran

It begins as joyous news. A nursery is planned. We have nine months to dream the baby's room into being. We bring in a new crib. We select a crib bumper. We prop stuffed animals on the diaper-changing table. We paint the room pastels. Then, we stand back, satisfied at this little bit of heaven on earth, a place where love will grow. It is a sweet and satisfying moment. Everything is in order, waiting for the child's arrival.

And it is the last moment that we will have complete control over that room, because the room reflects the child. The miracle of children is how very much they are their own person. As they change, the room will change with them. This is how it starts: the diaper table will be strewn with onesies covered in spit-up. The sweet stuffed animals will be knocked to the floor during a sleep-deprived feeding and diaper change when you couldn't find the baby wipes in the dark.

In two years, the pastel walls will be covered in red crayon marks. In seven years the floor will be covered in Legos. In ten years, you will be tripping over seven volumes of *Harry Potter*. In fifteen years, you will need to knock on the door to gain entry to that room—and if you manage to peek past the teenage sentry who is blocking the doorway, you'll see a vast array of clothing tossed to the floor, textbooks in a toppled pile, and the stray empty potato chip bag that was snuck into the room during an all-night homework or Skype session.

Children grow and change. It's not only in the nature of who they are, but it's also what we want for them. Growth is a constant. If we can live in the moment with our children, we will be able to see and celebrate their changes. We can be available compassionately during the inevitable growing pains.

There are two things that can pull us out of the moment with our children: the past and the future. If we focus too much on the past, we may get caught up in guilt and regret. We may also feel unrealistic nostalgia about our child's younger days. If we focus too much on the future, we may be trapped by worry. We might project our own unrealized dreams onto them—more like pressure than hope for their future.

Our children's rooms should be a reflection and a celebration of who they are in this moment. It is tempting to want to hang on to reminders of the child they once were, like clothing that no longer fits or toys they no longer play with. We also keep books that never sparked their imaginations and kits for hobbies that never triggered an interest—things that are more a testament to our hopes than to theirs.

In our hearts, we can't hold on to the smaller person this child once was. We can't view them through the lens of what we hope they will someday become. To do so is to ignore the human being that is blossoming right before our eyes. Ignorance of who our children are can do damage to their hearts and to the soul and spirit of our relationship with them.

The Spiritual Importance of Your Child's Room

Children do not see clutter. It does not register with them. If you point it out to them, they simply cannot see the problem with it—even if you explain. Your children do not understand your need for order and simplicity, which may give you the idea that they are openly defying you. They're not. So if you find yourself in a constant power struggle with your child because you believe that the way she keeps her room is an open act of rebellion and disrespect—and you are taking that as a personal affront, or see it as a disregard for everything you have sacrificed to make her happy—you can stop now. Seriously. *Stop*.

It's not personal. It's not rebellion. It's not disrespect, disregard, or ingratitude.

When Lauren was a child, her bedroom was the worst kind of chaotic wreck. (Yes, the very same Lauren who is coauthoring this book on decluttering.) Her parents were pulling their hair out. "How can you live like this?" they wailed. Lauren remembers looking around her room and honestly wondering, "What's their problem? I'm perfectly happy in here. Why can't they just let me be happy?"

So where is the disconnect? For adults, physical clutter is a manifestation of their internal clutter—consuming emotions and indecision. But for children, cluttering is a natural result of the powerful blossoming of consciousness. If someone has been walking the planet for less

than one or two decades, they are still wide-eyed. They are not trying
to order life or make sense of it. They are in it, absorbing every bit of
life—taking in what works, tossing what doesn't. They're exploring,
searching, and wondering. The result of this vast emotional, intellectual, and spiritual openness to life? That's right. Mess. Clutter. But it's
not a testament to a negative mental state; it's evidence of their positive emotional, intellectual, and spiritual condition.

Now we're both parents too, so if you think we are saying, "Just
leave your kids alone. Their mess and their clutter is not a problem,"
you are dead wrong. Children need to live in balance with the needs
of their family, because in addition to being these wide-eyed wonder-
filled star children, they also happen to be extremely egocentric. If
it's not a problem for them, they can't see why it's a problem for you.
Literally. According to Jean Piaget in *The Psychology of the Child*, children's brains will not allow them to witness the world from another
person's perspective. Part of parenting is to help them develop empathy and learn to see life through other people's eyes. Eventually they
will be adults; we must teach them empathy now, and teach them to
get organized and decluttered, so they have the skills they need when
their brains finally mature.

This is the lesson: we must see the child for who she is as we
witness the woman she is becoming—simultaneously. It's spiritual
visioning, like seeing the flower inside the tree and the mighty oak in
the acorn. It's all there, held in potential. Waiting to blossom. Waiting
to take root. And you, as parent, are tilling the soil and watering the
seed. So teach your child to declutter. Just don't expect it to stay that
way, and don't expect them to value it in the least. Your child's adult
self will thank you down the line. In fact, that adult self is already
there in seed form, waiting to hand you a thank-you note. Trust that.
And keep watering.

Releasing Attachments and Making Room for Growth: Kelly and Luna's Story

Kelly is touring me through her yard. Over here is the tree house, over there the organic garden. Kelly is the quintessential earth mother. And Luna is her beloved and beautiful daughter.

"I feel like in so many ways, I have been able to model for Luna what it means to be a good person. I'm spiritual, so I am able to show her how to be spiritual. I'm loving, so I am able to show her how to be loving. I'm kind, so I am able to show her how to be kind."

I nod and smile, observing their wordless bond as they walk through the yard together. Spiritual. Loving. Kind: this is absolutely true of both of them.

"But when it comes to decluttering," Kelly says with a sigh, "I have no idea how to show her how to do that, because *I* don't know how do that."

This, too, is true. As we walk from room to room in Kelly's home, it's clear that she does not know how to say "no" to anything. Though she holds down a day job at a local medical laboratory to help support her family, she is an artist and a crafter at heart. Everything she touches speaks to her of some new possibility. As we look around her home, I count no less than four crafting areas, all filled to bursting with crafting supplies, fabric scraps, and found objects—all of which Kelly has every intention of turning into something beautiful. Kelly clearly ascribes to the crafter's motto: "I could use that!" Unfortunately, this is a clutterer's motto, as well.

And still, their house is full of examples of their creative charm and their mutual delight in beauty. Kelly shows me their family altar, with photos and mementos celebrating the love they share together.

After touring the house, I suggest we work together in eleven-year-old Luna's bedroom, which is covered corner-to-corner with toys, dolls, stuffed animals, clothing, books, and art projects. The child has her mother's zest for life and penchant for the seeing the possibilities in everything. Every surface, shelf, and chair is covered with small worlds created with dolls, furniture, scarves, and figurines.

"I love that she is still very much a little girl. She's still very naïve and childlike. I want to preserve that innocence in her for as long as I can," says Kelly.

I understand. To mothers, it can feel like a treacherous world out there. Kelly's concerns are real. Little girls grow up fast these days and are encouraged by the media to shed their little-girl ways early. Peer pressure is very intense—and the internet and social media make it all-too-easy for young children to be exposed to confusing, upsetting images and ideas. This is not an easy world to navigate. It is very tempting to want to shelter our children completely.

At the same time, children *do* grow up. Trying to keep them small and completely protect them from the wiles and temptations of the outside world is futile. The question is not "Will they grow up?" but "How will they grow up?" All parents must consider what kind of adults we want our children to become. There is no time like the present to start answering those kinds of questions.

So I begin with an unusual question—at least not one you would expect from a professional declutterer: "What is it that you want to be when you grow up, Luna?"

"I want to be a designer," she says with absolute certainty.

"Awesome," I say. And I mean it. That answer is going to guide our work together. We are going to make room for the designer in Luna to emerge and take flight.

Dr. Green Weighs In on Kelly and Luna's Clutter

It's incredibly sweet (and remarkably self-aware) that Kelly does not want to pass along her habits to her daughter. She knows how much frustration and overwhelm her ways have introduced into her life. She wants her daughter to know a better way. Psychologically speaking, she is not just doing this for her daughter; she is doing this for her own inner girl. Kelly missed out on an opportunity to learn something essential about keeping life clean and simple, and she is determined to learn it alongside her daughter.

Kelly is also facing another issue that all parents take on: How do we affirm and protect our children, while stepping aside and making room for their growth? How can we be available to guide that growth in a healthy way? Kelly needs to create space for Luna to develop into the woman she is to become.

Luna is on the edge of puberty. Her mother is well aware that she is about to go through an awesome transition. Parents of boys know that their sons are about to undergo similar physical, emotional, and spiritual transformations. Native cultures celebrate these rites of passage, but in our modern culture, we tend to sweep these changes under the rug. There is a sense of shame about the way the body is changing. At the same time, advertisements and television shows objectify the developing bodies of young teens and glorify these changes in totally inappropriate, damaging ways. So instead of a passing into maturity in safe ritual container, children are left to their own devices. They explore their changes in a culture that seeks to sensationalize and degrade these changes. This is the source of the danger that Kelly and other parents like her are fearful of.

A rite of passage is about ritually letting go of the old in order to invite the new. Kelly wants to teach her daughter to be a woman in a healthy way—with self-respect and self-love. In order to do this, she must allow and even encourage Luna to let go of what no longer serves her spirit.

If we give into the dualistic social construct that naïveté is safe and growth is dangerous, then we are shutting down the possibility of an evolving conversation that includes a safe, whole, and healthy approach to growth. Decluttering with our children is an opportunity to allow that conversation to blossom.

Lauren Teaches Luna (and Kelly) to Declutter

"If you are going to be a designer, then you'll need a place to design."

"I have this desk," says Luna, shrugging, "but there's nowhere to work on it." She's correct. Her desk is covered in clutter.

"Okay," I say to mother and daughter, "Luna has made her intention clear that she wants to be a designer. Our work is to liberate the space for that to happen. So, usually when organizers come into a home they ask, 'Do you use this? Do you want to donate this? Trash it? Sell it?' I have a different set of questions for Luna. As we sort through the contents of this desk, we are going to ask the question: *Does this represent who you are right now, who you want to be in the future, or who you were in the past?*

"If it represents who she is right now as a developing artist, it stays on the desk. If it represents the young woman she wants to become, then it also stays. If it represents who she was in the past, then we have to ask another set of questions: *Is this a significant symbol of who you were in the past? Or is it an insignificant item?*

"Now, we are going to create room on a shelf in Luna's room for significant symbols of who she once was. We don't want to throw away her childhood. We want to honor it, but we don't need it to take up active space. Is all that clear?"

They both nod, and we get to work. Luna is amazingly decisive about what represents her past, her present, or her future. She is lightning quick to decide which things are significant and which are insignificant. She has no problem throwing insignificant things in the trash bag or the to-donate pile. Kelly is amazed at how clear and decisive Luna is. "I've tried decluttering with her in the past, but I've always asked her, 'Are you attached to this?' We never get anywhere!"

"It's the wrong question," I tell Kelly. "The answer to 'Are you attached to this?' is always going to be yes. If you didn't have an attachment to it, you wouldn't have it. The more important question to ask is, 'How does this serve who you are and who you are choosing to become?' It's a really important question for all of us to ask, no matter what age we are."

Soon, Luna's desk is cleared, and we position a reading lamp above it. A cup holding markers and pencils sits to the side, and just next to it is a neat stack of paper, awaiting the brilliant strokes of Luna's imagination. We've cleared a space on the floor and moved a chair up to the desk. Luna's inner designer is about to take off. She's smiling from ear to ear.

As Luna and I admire her design station, Kelly disappears. When she returns a minute later, she has a homemade doll in her arms. "This is mine," she says as she touches the doll's faded yarn hair. "My aunt made it for me back when Cabbage Patch Dolls were popular. I've always had a hard time imagining letting her go, but I think I am ready to let her go now. Do you think you could take her for me, though?"

"Are you sure?" I ask.

"Yes," she answers, gently handing the doll to me.

"Okay. I'll donate her. And I promise you that some little girl will be overjoyed to find her."

"Wait," says Kelly. She reaches out and removes a tiny hospital bracelet from the doll's arm. "I'll keep this as a reminder," she says, tucking it into her pocket and smiling. "It's significant."

This is the kind of moment that makes me so happy that I do what I do: Luna has learned how to declutter in order to make room for her inner woman to blossom. Kelly has taught her inner child to let go.

I hug them both as I prepare to leave. I tell them how proud I am of both of them. And I am—I really am.

✳ 🏠 ♥

Possible Intention Words for Your Child's Room

Enjoyable. Fun. Creative. Focused. Familiar. Growth. Encouraging. Bright. Easy. Relaxing. Stimulating. Friendship. Happy. Joyful. Lively. Restful. Inspiring. Inquisitive. Supported. Interesting.

A Blessing for Your Child's Room

May this room be filled with love and creativity, joy and growth. May I peek into this room, with all its clutter and mess and chaos, and give thanks for a child who is healthy, whole, and full of wonder. May I have the strength to see through my child's troubles—with patience and compassion—for I was once a child and needed those things. May I celebrate growth and be there to guide it. This room will not be occupied for long. If I do my job well and fill my child's heart with confidence, love, and security, the day will come when they will leave this room and wave good-bye. So for now, I pour my love into this room. I fill it with light. I surround it with safety. I look for the blessings within. Even the mess. Even the clutter. Every sock, shoe, marker, doll, and toy car is an opportunity to teach my child to embrace what is true and to release what is not. May they always continue down the path of love knowing how to do just this.

An Exercise for Teaching Your Child to Declutter

Honestly, the best way to teach your child to declutter is not by demanding it of them, but by showing them how it's done. Children (especially as they approach their teen years) have a low tolerance for hypocrisy. They can spot it a mile away, we assure you. So if you ask them to declutter their space but you are not decluttering yours, the hypocrisy alarm will go off. The problem is, many of us were never taught how to declutter, so we may very well be at a loss to teach our children.

Most children don't like to clean. They don't like to declutter. It's a well-established fact (at least in our homes). Kids are perfectly happy living in chaos, hopping through an obstacle course of clothing, discarded toys, and board games left in mid-play. We tell them the reward for cleaning your room is having a clean room. Most children, when you say something like this, will look at you like you are from Mars—but not quite as excited as they might be about a Martian. They don't really value having a neat room, so they don't see it as a reward for the time and energy they are being asked to expend.

Now, of course, once the room is actually clean, they might feel quite happy and proud. They may—unless they are in a brutally foul mood from being forced to clean—even enjoy being in their room more. But on the front end—the "I'd like you to pick up your room" end—this is a hard sell.

The first thing we need to do is release our judgment. Children become resistant and will dig their heels in when they feel judged. Make the goal small. Insisting that the whole thing gets done and then closing the door never works. In fact, what you will usually find is you will come back thirty minutes later to either find them sulking in the exact same place or happily playing with their toys in the midst of the mess.

Start small, and make the reward clear:

"Let's clean out this drawer together and then we can take a walk."

"Let's go through these old clothes. If we can find twenty things you don't wear anymore we'll donate them, and you can get that *Star Wars* t-shirt you wanted."

"Let's go through this toy closet and find the toys that you don't play with anymore. While we drive to the donation center, we can turn on your favorite radio station."

It's important to remember you are teaching through small successes the value, ease, and reward of a job well done. Your child needs one small, accomplishable job at a time. She needs happy, supportive company in the process. She needs acknowledgment and reward when she is finished.

The goal is to enjoy the process and learn the inherent reward of having a decluttered space. Since recent research shows that the human brain does not reach its full adult maturity until a person is in his or her mid-twenties,[1] it may be quite a while before your children genuinely appreciate a decluttered living space. But when they do get there, they'll know how to do it, because you've taught them joyfully.

Note:

1. Tony Cox, "Brain Maturity Extends Well Beyond Teen Years: An Interview with Neuroscientist Sandra Aamodt," *npr.org*, October 10, 2011, http://www.npr.org /templates/story/story.php?storyId=141164708.

10

....

Your Home Office:
Room for Information
and Inspiration

My desk drawer is filled with all kinds of prayers.
—GERALDINE FERRARO

We all have the places we like to go to get our work done. Some of us like to work in the open, in common areas: at the kitchen counter, the dining room table, the coffee table next to the couch. We like to be in the thick of things when we work; we're inspired by the movement and the chatter. It increases our creative flow. It lessens our anxiety. Others like to be tucked away where we can focus without distraction. Our home offices and studios are very personal spaces that reflect the way we like to get our work done, whether our work is paying bills; writing essays; communicating with colleagues, friends, and family; or creating collages. Yet, if we are not careful, these workspaces, whether they are in the middle of the dining room table or tucked away in a corner of the attic, can easily become cluttered spaces that reflect our anxieties more than our passions—our dysfunction more than our functionality.

Piles upon piles of envelopes, flyers, business cards; reminders of what to do, what to schedule, what to file, and what to pay—the home office, whether it is a room unto itself or a desk in the corner, is frequently a space that vibrates with an overwhelming sense of anxiety—even panic. The home office can feel as if it is filled to bursting with papers, and all the fears and stressors these things carry with them. It is more than a little tempting to bar the door to this room altogether.

Yet, an office has the potential to be the room through which energetic abundance of money, life, and creativity flow.

The Spiritual Importance of Your Home Office

When we were researching this book, we asked people to rate their level of clutter on a scale of 0 to 10, with 0 being "It's practically a Zen monastery" and 10 being "It's so cluttered it's unsafe." People consistently rated their home office or studio as one of their most cluttered rooms. We think there are a couple reasons why. The first reason is that our offices are private. They're not a public space, so we can hide them from view without fear of being judged.

The second reason is that our workspaces can make us feel anxious. They can bring up serious questions about our competence and our value in the world. They can also bring up anxieties about losing track of important details of our lives: bank statements, calendars, and to-do lists.

Fear of being judged. Fear of being incompetent. Anxiety that what we need to function is slipping away from us. Put these things together and they spell "clutter." Yet the more we avoid the clutter, the greater our fear and anxiety can grow. There could not be a clearer example of inner clutter generating external clutter.

Most of what we do in our offices falls into the category "thankless tasks." This means tasks that we pour energy into that yield no joyful reward. And what do we call things we pour our energy into but that we get nothing out of? Yes, we call those tasks "consuming."

If you keep a home studio, you may also be hiding your work from the world. Art represents the soul—at once the most powerful and most sensitive piece of our being. Just as we have fears around our thankless tasks, we also have fears around our soul work: What if I pour out my soul and no one understands it? What if I express who I am and no one likes it? What if *I* don't like it? There's lots to hide here too.

But not all work-related fears are created equal. They can be deeply seated self-doubt, as we've described. It can also be a nagging sense of anxiety that we are drowning in a sea of paperwork, sticky notes, to-do lists, receipts, and appointments. Even a small pile of unsorted papers on a desk can become a source of avoidance if we have the nagging anxiety that there is something missing in that pile that could be the source of our undoing: a bill left unpaid for too long, an invitation to a birthday party that we may have missed, a reminder for a doctor's appointment that we forgot. Even the smallest amount of work-related anxiety can snowball. The more anxious we feel, the more we'll avoid the clutter; the more we avoid it, the more clutter will build; and as more clutter accumulates, the greater our anxiety and avoidance. And so it goes.

So, whether your workspace creates a deep fear or a superficial anxiety, we have one word for you: courage. Okay, two words: courage and perseverance. We have to have the courage to face our fears, and really look at them. We will never know what we are made of until we do this. If we are constantly retreating from the thing that frightens us, then we will not know how heroic we truly are. Have you ever considered that your hero's journey might lead across the surface of your desk? Or right up to your easel?

No more hiding. No more refusing to face your fears. True spiritual warriors look their fears in the eyes and say, "Let me show you what I'm made of!"

Say this to your bills, taxes, paints, clay, or that empty page in your journal that is just waiting for you to write the first line of your novel! Say it fearlessly!

Go get 'em, tiger!

✳   🏠   ♥

Decluttering Distraction and Making Room for What Matters: Jennifer's Story

Jennifer and her husband, Bob, are both art and design aficionados. Indeed, their home—spacious, light infused, and filled with uplifting and quirky works of modern art—looks like something you would see in *Architectural Digest* magazine. Displayed throughout their home are mementos of their world travels, taken with their three school-aged children. Their collection is placed tastefully throughout the home they designed and built just two years before.

When I arrive, Jennifer invites me to a room off her kitchen so she can make me a cappuccino. "Bob and I went to 'Espresso University' when we lived in Tuscany with the kids. We learned the precise number of seconds that is optimal to create the perfect foam—it's twenty-three seconds, by the way." As she hands me my cappuccino (which is the best I've ever tasted, and I tell her so; "It's the way I pack in the grounds," she says and winks), she apologizes for not creating a picture in the foam. "This is two percent milk. Foam art works better with whole milk."

The tour of their home reveals treasures that are as bright, fun, and delightful as Jennifer's sweet and sunny personality. She is quick to laugh as she shows me a lamp on the wall. "Touch the bulb," she tells me. When I reach out, it isn't a bulb at all, but a hologram. Amazing.

A tour of the yard shows me an infinity pool with a fountain. A trip to the living room reveals a flat-screen TV that descends from the ceiling to cover a large painting hung over the mantel. Another touch of a button and the TV vanishes back into the ceiling and the painting is once again front and center. "Bob wanted a TV in the living room. I didn't want TV to be the focus. This was our compromise. Cool, huh?" She grins mischievously.

But suddenly we are not looking at cool gadgets, dreamy landscapes, soul-stirring art, or mind-bending optical illusions. Jennifer takes me into the small office space that she calls her "command central." We are looking at a small brass washer, about the size of a child's pinky nail. We found it, along with a handful of other spare parts, in a small container in the desk drawer.

"What does this belong to?" I ask.

Suddenly, Jennifer's smile disappears and her brow knits. "I don't know. I don't know how long I've been holding on to it. At least a couple of years, if not more. I keep waiting to figure out what it belongs to."

"Then we can throw it out?" I ask. I am hoping she is game.

But she's not. "As soon I throw it out, I'm going to find the thing that it belongs to."

I can see what a challenge this is for her—her fear is that there are missing pieces of the puzzle. So I try to counter with a bit of professional declutterer's logic: "For two years, you have had this missing part in your possession. That means for two years you have been living without the thing it belongs to, right?"

"Right," she says with an eyebrow raised. She is following me, but I can see that she fears I am leading her into an ambush. "So?"

"So if there has been no noticeable impact on your life, it is highly unlikely that this thing—whatever it is—is a life-saving device."

"I get your point," she says. She takes a deep breath, steeling herself. Letting her breath out slowly, she opens up her hand. "Okay, I guess we can throw it out."

With that, she opens up her hand and lets the little brass washer tumble into the trash can. She smiles, and I can see the relief on her face. "Although, you know," she says with a genuine laugh, smile lines breaking around her sparkling eyes, "tomorrow I'm going to figure out what that belonged to."

Jennifer lives with a constant fear that she is losing pieces of the big picture. By her own admission, every single day feels like an improvisation to her. She says, "No one day looks like the next. I just get through any way I can." For some people, that might feel like an adventure. For Jennifer, it is a source of anxiety that preys on her. She feels like she can't find what she needs when she needs it. She feels like she spends an inordinate amount of time hunting for papers and objects that the day demands.

Ironically, the reason Jennifer can't find what she needs is that she worries about throwing anything away that might end up being important. Her fear makes it virtually impossible for her to find anything that is important.

It's a very typical clutterer's conundrum.

Dr. Green Weighs In on Jennifer's Clutter

Often, people who have a zest for life and believe anything is possible can be quite distractible. Every shining possibility pulls at their attention. Every opportunity is a new project. If they were focused on one thing and see something else glimmering in the distance, they can't help but tear off in the direction of the new possibility. It can be quite attractive and child-like, this tendency to see new possibilities blooming everywhere.

The trouble comes where nothing ever gets finished because everything is in process. The appeal of the new is much more alluring than following through. Over time, piles and piles of unfinished and half finished projects accumulate. Worry builds on top of that, because nothing is prioritized. Nothing takes precedence. Everything is calling out at the same volume and it can be confusing and worrisome and maddening.

People who are naturally creative sometimes suffer from what I might call "possibility addiction." Projects lose their appeal once they are started. There might be long, boring stretches in the process of seeing the project through. There may be challenges along the way. That is not nearly as fun as imagining possibility. When we commit to one thing, we are by nature saying no to something else. That can be hard too: saying no to some possibilities in favor of others.

My recommendation for Jennifer—and people like her who are full of life and who love the possible—is to create a process for looking at what's possible and set limits on how long possibilities are allowed to linger. By limiting the number of possibilities that come into view, she is allowing for her priorities to manifest powerfully. This will relieve the anxiety caused by being at sea in an ocean of possibility.

Lauren's Decluttering Session with Jennifer

After our tour of the house, Jennifer decides that we will declutter her "command central" station. Her fear of losing track of what she needs in life centers around this area. She says she feels anxious and claustrophobic.

When I ask her what words she would like to focus on as intentions as we declutter, Jennifer chooses *shared, open, future-focused, efficient, effective,* and *communicative.* I write the words down on a sticky note so we can pin it to the bulletin board.

"Coffees," she says quietly. I look at her quizzically. The coffees we drank are now drained and the cups are in the kitchen sink. She sees my confusion and explains, "What you wrote on the paper: the acronym is COFFEES. Communicative. Open. Future-Focused. Efficient. Effective. Shared. I'm good at word games." She shrugs.

"Wow." I nod in appreciation, impressed.

This woman is sharp. She gets it. She doesn't want to be worried or anxious. I write her acronym on a larger piece of paper and replace the original sticky note. If anything is going to stick—it's this clever acronym. She doesn't identify with these positive feelings, so she is preparing to declutter everything that is getting in the way of her COFFEES intention. Anything that does not resonate within the intentions of that acronym—goes.

When we finish, we have cleared the desktop that was piled high with papers. Jennifer's bulletin board (now featuring a calendar and a weekly to-do list) is divided into three sections: *this month, next month,* and *beyond next month.* We reserve a space on the bulletin board for her children's art.

All the possibilities are still there, but they are out in clear view. Nothing is hidden or lost. No worry, fear, or anxiety.

"How do you feel?" I ask when we are finished.

"I feel like I have room to breathe," she says, beaming.

She does. And that is exactly the point.

Possible Intention Words for Your Home Office

Focused. Communicative. Sharing. Fluid. Flow. Creative. Inspired. Inspirational. Fearless. Courageous. Daring. Enjoyable. Abundant.

Rich. Insightful. Healing. Connective. Vibrant. Intuitive. Collaborative. Informative.

A Blessing for Your Home Office

May this room be blessed with abundance—abundant joy, abundant wealth, abundant wisdom, and abundant creativity. May I learn to say "thank you" to my thankless tasks so that I may see that no activity is devoid of spiritual lessons. Everything is sacred, even my bills, my taxes, my writer's block, and the empty canvas. May I know myself to be a true spiritual warrior and face my fears in this room so I might clear the blockages that are preventing true spiritual energy and Divine light to flow through this space.

An Exercise for Decluttering Your Home Office

You probably already have the habit of sorting through the clutter in your office and separating it into keep/recycle/throw away piles. We want you to try something a little different.

We want you to lay out a number line on the floor of your space with the numbers 1 through 10. One represents the things that you are not the least bit afraid of touching, sorting, or dealing with. Ten represents the things that terrify you.

How much of your work falls at 1? How much falls at 10? Is there an organizing principle here? Is there a common denominator between the things that cluster around 1 and those that are gathered around 10?

Over the next ten days, you are going to build your courage. On day one, you are going to sort, touch, and deal with your 1s, work

with the 2s on day two, and so on. You are going to make clear decisions about which items you need to take action on, which items get
filed, and which items need to be decluttered by being sent to the
trash or the recycling. At the end of each day, you are going to reflect
on the work you've done.

Here are a few guiding sample prompts for your journal entry:

On day one, I sorted through and decluttered the following items:
What these things had in common:
The feelings I had when I sorted through this pile were:
The inner resources I used for this work were:
In the end, I had these feelings:
I feel strong, courageous, and competent because:

As you work over the next ten days, take note of the inner
resources you are gathering and feel how you're building your courage. We learn what we are capable of by testing our capabilities. This
exercise of your native courage will teach you that there is nothing
you are hiding from that you can't ultimately face.

11

....

Your Bedroom:
Room for Rest and Love

*We cultivate love when we allow our most vulnerable and
powerful selves to be deeply seen and known, and when we honor
the spiritual connection that grows from that offering with trust,
respect, kindness, and affection.*

—BRENÉ BROWN

If our homes were temples, our bedrooms would be the holy of
holies, private spaces where we are most deeply vulnerable. In other
rooms we might play a role: cook, host, entertainer, manager, artist.
But in the bedroom, among scattered pillows and tangled sheets, we
are simply ourselves: tousled, tired, releasing ourselves to the mys-
terious tales of the unconscious mind—releasing ourselves, perhaps,
to love and being loved. You may share your bedroom with another
person, or it may be your private sanctuary. In either case, this is still
the place in your home where each night you let go of your plans
and give yourself over to dreams. Here, you wake each morning
to renewed consciousness and awareness. It is the place where you
meet yourself, your beloved, and each new day. The bedroom is your
inner sanctum.

We get it: you're tired. Your days are exhausting. You have so many responsibilities to attend to; so many people count on you. From the time your alarm clock goes off, you give your very best all day long. It's not easy. When all is said and done, you just want to toss your clothes on the floor, crawl under your covers, lay your weary head down, shut your eyes, and call it a day.

What a missed opportunity!

Your bedroom is more than just a room to collapse in at the end of the day. Your bedroom is a garden of love, relaxation, and restoration.

But most of us don't treat our bedrooms this way. Perhaps we are afraid of love's impermanence. We avoid the vulnerability that is required of us. We're embarrassed by being nakedly honest (or just plain *naked*). So instead of cultivating our emotional garden, we trash it. Our bedrooms become dumping grounds for the dregs of our daily lives. We stash objects and emotions we either don't know how to handle or don't have the energy for. We tune in to our televisions and turn off our emotions, taking our lives and partners for granted. We carry our work to bed, along with our computers and our smartphones. We read our emails, check our bank balances, obsessively track the most disturbing news stories of the day—and then we wonder why we can't seem to communicate with the person we love or why we have trouble sleeping.

The good news is that your bedroom is not a paradise lost. It is a paradise waiting to be found, uncovered, and cultivated—a paradise waiting to be decluttered and revealed.

The Spiritual Importance of Your Bedroom

We all need refuge. It's a physical, emotional, and spiritual necessity. And we all need love. It does not matter whether you are in a relationship or not. Humans need to receive love in order to feel truly at home.

So even if you are in a relationship, you must learn to offer yourself love and care first. If we are completely dependent on a partner or spouse for love and care, it creates a lot of pressure in a relationship.

One of the key ways we can offer love to ourselves—and truly receive it—is to allow ourselves full and complete rest. Total surrender. Our bodies, minds, and spirits have inner wisdom. We need to let our guard down, release the day, and allow for full rejuvenation. Not allowing ourselves rest or relaxation is a form of self-abuse. This work of decluttering is about worthiness. You are worthy of self-love and self-care.

If your bedroom is so cluttered that it prohibits you from fully receiving these things, it is time to ask yourself some important questions:

What are you afraid of? What do you think will happen if you let your guard down? What stories are you telling yourself about the necessity of guarding yourself against disaster? There is no disaster equal to a life that doesn't allow love. So, staying up late into the night worrying about your car payments, your next big meeting, how the laundry is going to get done, and how you are going to confront the neighbor about his barking dog is not preventing disaster—it's creating it.

It's time to declutter your bedroom and make room for the love and rest you deserve.

Decluttering Trauma and Making Room for Trust: Elena's Story

When I walk into Elena's home, she has a phone balanced on her shoulder. She is talking with a drywall contractor about fixing the downstairs ceiling.

It was destroyed when a pipe sprung a leak while she, her partner, and her three children were on vacation. As she irons out the final details on the call, she holds up one index finger to me to indicate that she is almost done.

After she hangs up, she gives me a hug. "I'm so glad you're here. To be honest, I almost canceled this appointment," she says. She looks up to the place where the ceiling used to be and sighs. "There's so much craziness going on in this house." She lets out a deep breath. "And then I realized that I was just using this as an excuse. I think I'm really afraid of what I might find once I start going through this house."

Elena feels that in the last several years, her life has been like moving from one trauma to the next, with never a chance to catch her breath. In fact, her relationship with her current partner, Joseph (the father of one of her three children; they're not married), was forged in the wake of her divorce from her first husband, Ty. Joseph and Elena were best friends, and when Elena realized that her marriage was unraveling—and that she was about to be a single mother of two children—Joseph was the rock she could really lean on. Following Elena's divorce, her friendship with Joseph deepened. They began to meet every Tuesday over jasmine tea. Joseph wrote Elena letters telling her how much he admired her. How strong she was. And how beautiful. Those letters became love letters. Their friendship grew into love. Not long after, Elena became pregnant with Joseph's child. They built this house and started a life together.

But it was never easy. Ty, a world traveler, is in and out of their lives. He visits his two children between his stays in foreign lands, always bringing back presents to the children. The kids adore Ty and admire him for his adventurous spirit and sense of fun; Elena's oldest child began to resent Joseph, whose insistence that the young boy do his chores made him seem dull and oppressive. Even when he isn't there, Ty is a constant presence in the house, a child's ideal parent: fun and permissive, leading an exotic life of intrigue. In comparison, the dad who now lives in the home asks the kids to pick up their socks, water the plants, and walk the dog. The tension between Joseph and Elena's oldest son is palpable. Elena started to worry that her relationship with Joseph was destined to end as well, and that she would be a single mother again, this time with *three* children. No wonder Elena was afraid for me to take a look into her home.

We decide that we will work on decluttering Elena and Joseph's bedroom. Looking out onto a peaceful green meadow dotted with wildflowers, the room is a romantic paradise. A large window with a spacious view sits across from the bed. French doors open out to a deck with two chairs, side by side. Near the French doors is a chaise longue with a little reading table. It's technically a very romantic setup, but it doesn't feel the least bit romantic. The chaise longue is draped with their youngest daughter's rumpled blanket; two of her stuffed animals lie on the floor next to it. The view beyond the large, gorgeous window is blocked by a model ship that belonged to Joseph's father.

"I can't stand that thing," Elena mutters, shaking her head. When I ask her how frequently she and Joseph enjoy the deck together, she looks sheepish. "I'm embarrassed to tell you. Never."

I ask Elena to visualize her beloved as she sets her intention for the room. She closes her eyes and puts her hand over her heart. I can see clearly how much she truly loves Joseph. Her face relaxes and the corners of her mouth turn up into a peaceful smile. She sways gently with her eyes closed, as if she were dancing in his arms. She does not open her eyes as she says, "Love. Connection. Romance." She opens her eyes and looks around the room. "You know, when we painted this room, we chose a color called Soul Mate. It's fitting, you know? Because that's what we are: soul mates." We add those words to her intention.

As we begin to move around the room, looking for objects that don't fit with her intention, I discover a jar of money, about seventy dollars in bills and change. I ask Elena why she has it. She shakes her head. "I guess I've been stashing money in that jar in case things don't work out with Joseph. I thought, 'Well, if I ever have to be on my own again, I'll have my own money.'" When she looks at me, I can tell we are having the same thought. "As I am telling this to you, I realize that there is barely enough money for a single shopping trip in here."

"Elena?" I say, trying to catch her eye. "It may be a little inappropriate for you to keep your getaway money in the bedroom you share with the man you've made a life with."

She bursts into laughter. "Oh my gosh! I never thought of it that way!"

Dr. Green Weighs In on Elena's Clutter

Because she is traumatized by the unraveling of her previous relationship, Elena is afraid to relax into her current relationship. She suffered the last time her relationship collapsed, so she is constantly preparing herself for another blow. It is like the way we tense up when we are falling. We're trying to prepare for the impact, but ultimately the tension in our bodies may end up causing more harm; if we just relaxed, the fall wouldn't have hurt us.

Elena has a deep-seated fear that her heart may be broken again, so she is pre-experiencing the heartbreak so she won't be taken by surprise by it, should it happen again. Unfortunately, when people are traumatized they often find themselves reliving the trauma again and again. Although she thinks she's shielding herself from heartbreak, Elena is actually setting the stage for it. She literally has one foot out the door.

This relationship has no chance at succeeding until Elena looks with deep compassion at her previous trauma. She has to relax into this new relationship and allow the trust to build. The lack of trust she feels toward Joseph is not really directed at Joseph at all—it's directed toward Ty. Her ex-husband is a constant presence in her current relationship; she must release the past and forgive, so she can truly live in the present with her beloved. There are always risks involved in any loving relationship, including the risk of being hurt. There is no absolute safety. But if we are constantly braced for pain, love and trust don't have a snowball's chance.

Lauren Helps Elena Declutter Her Bedroom

Elena and I started by identifying objects that have nothing to do with soul mates, love, connection, or romance. We remove an army of children's toys, blankets, and books. We toss out work-related materials, the model ship, and another jar of money. (Elena blushes. "Geez, I forgot this one was in here!")

But that's not all. We find quite a few things that belonged to Ty: a childhood photo of Ty and his brother. Two of his childhood toys. In the desk in the corner of the bedroom, we find a checkbook from their joint checking account and her wedding ring—it had broken into two pieces. ("Symbolic, huh?" Elena says.) Ty is all over their bedroom. But now, Elena is intent on getting him out. She knows it is time to let her first marriage go. She is aware that the survival of her current relationship depends on that.

Then, we find a treasure. In the same desk are the love letters that Joseph had written to Elena as their friendship magically turned to love. She lays them out on the bed, where previously there had been a business book and a stuffed animal.

"I think we'll read these together tonight," she says. She gazes out the window. "I think I know what I am going to put in that window now. I'm going to get a jasmine plant, for the jasmine tea we drank together when we first realized we were falling in love."

I see Elena's eyes fill up with tears.

She tells me, "I feel like I know what I want for the first time in years. I feel like I've been just going from one crisis to another, ever since my marriage to Ty ended. In all that time, I never stopped to ask myself what it was I really wanted. And I want Joseph." She paused for a moment to wipe her eyes. "And I want to thank you, because I feel like you just saved my relationship."

Possible Intention Words for Your Bedroom

Restful. Relaxing. Loving. Supportive. Intimate. Gentle. Connective. Intuitive. Sweetness. Ease. Refuge. Communication. Kindness. Simplicity. Acceptance. Surrender. Open. Joyful. Healing. Appreciative.

A Blessing for Your Bedroom

May this bedroom be a haven of peace and a refuge of love. May I find within these walls perfect rest in the arms of the Divine. May the love shared here be an expression of that first, perfect love—the love of the Divine, Holy Oneness for Creation. May my worries vanish like mist in the sunshine of pure love. May the Moon shine her tender light into this space, filling it with gentleness and kindness. May I rest in her light and be safe. May my dreams lead me down the path to insight. May I arise wiser and stronger every morning. May I carry the love and comfort I feel in this room out into the world each day, offering peace and safety to those whose lives I touch.

An Exercise for Decluttering Your Bedroom

Take a slow, meditative walk around your bedroom. As you walk, say this mantra: *This room is made for love. This room is made for connection. This room is made for rest.* With each repetition, you will feel more and more deeply the emotional states of love, connection, and inner peace. Each line of this mantra is said in two parts. One half is for your inhale. The next is for your exhale. Like this:

> This room (*in breath*) . . . is made for love (*out breath*)
> This room (*in breath*) . . . is made for connection (*out breath*)
> This room (*in breath*) . . . is made for peace (*out breath*)

As you walk around the room, notice the objects that reflect those loving feelings back to you. As you walk past these items, put your palms together in gratitude, smile, and silently thank these items for supporting you in love, connection, and peace. Feel free to pick up these objects and move them to a more prominent place in your room. If they are hidden or buried, move them to a place where they are in full view.

Also notice the objects that are not conducive to those feelings: objects that make you feel anxiety, worry, regret, anger. As with any difficult emotion, our goal is to face it. See if you can label the emotion attached to the object. Does it make you feel fearful, nervous, distracted, edgy, or angry? Ask yourself: Does this object belong in a room made for love? Is it the proper furnishing for a room for love? Can it be reimagined or transformed, or does it simply not belong?

12

Your Bathroom:
Room for Self-Acceptance
and Renewal

*Inside myself is a place where I live all alone,
and that's where I renew my springs that never dry up.*

—PEARL S. BUCK

Steam fills the air as the sound of rushing water hitting the tiles drowns out the noise of traffic outside the window, the voices drifting up the stairs, and the morning news blaring on the television in the adjoining room. Colorful bottles filled with cleansers and potions are balanced on every shelf, each with its own scent, texture, and promise of renewal. As you step into the shower, you can feel your thoughts washing away. For a few precious moments, you are like the water: clear, flowing, pure. This is the essential magic of the bathroom—the room created for self-acceptance and renewal.

There is nothing like the feeling of coming clean, washing away the dust and the buildup of the day. In our bathrooms, we are able to come back to the very basic elements of who we are—pure, clean, bare—just the way we enter and leave the world. Simple acceptance. No judgment. But too often, we use our bathrooms to judge ourselves. We stand in front of the mirror and hunt for imperfections. We look for wrinkles. We shake our heads at our dimpled thighs, spare tires, and thinning hair and wish we could be different: younger, thinner, more attractive, more fit. When we look in the mirror, we are less likely to see what we are and more likely to see what we are not. So we fill our bathrooms with all manner of creams, lotions, and cosmetics. We buy things to remove what is there, to enhance what's not there. Our bathrooms are filled with clutter that reflects our insecurities and reminds us that we are either too much of one thing or not enough of another.

The Spiritual Importance of Your Bathroom

Every heart needs cleansing and renewal, just as every body does. The care of the soul is just as crucial to our wellness as the care of the body; perhaps more so, because the body can thrive while the soul stagnates. The body can be purified while the soul becomes clouded and dingy.

The bathroom is the place we go to for solitude, alone time, and self-care. Within those walls, we see the fullness of our physicality—our naked selves, real and dimpled and sagging; our selves that pass waste; our selves that are filthy and in need of renewal; our renewed selves that rise up cleansed and refreshed. We are able to see the full spectrum of our humanity in our bathrooms. But the question is, are we really willing to see it all? Can we face ourselves in our fullness? Are we willing to see our own beauty in the mirror as we witness that we are aging? Are we willing to love ourselves, even when our bodies are far from society's arbitrary standard of perfection?

The bathroom is the place that we will see it all. If we want to embrace it all, without covering it up or running away, we have to have the patience and the willingness to truly be with ourselves. There is freedom in our daily solitude and beauty as we work on accepting what is not always beautiful.

✳   🏠   ♥

Decluttering Unworthiness and Making Room for Self Care: Lynette's Story

Lynette has been in crisis for most of her adult life. At twenty-three, she was diagnosed with Hodgkin's disease. Three years later, her mother, who she dearly loved, died suddenly of a heart attack, right after they'd taken a vacation together. At twenty-seven, still grieving, she reunited with a high-school classmate: an attractive man who had been very popular in high school; Lynette was thrilled to be on the receiving end of his attention at the reunion. Not believing that she was worthy of being courted romantically, she pursued him aggressively in the weeks and months following their reunion. After dating for five years, the two finally married, but once they moved in together, his charming personality changed altogether. Her new husband suffered from bipolar disorder and was verbally and emotionally abusive. She knew right away she had made a mistake. However, not understanding that she deserved to be treated with kindness and dignity (if not love) in a marriage, she endured. Three years later, they had their first child, a son.

Two years after that, they had a daughter. The following year, her son was diagnosed with autism. Four years later, Lynette and her husband finally divorced. Her ex-husband moved out of state and she found herself on her own with two children, one of whom had special needs. Lynette eventually moved back to her hometown with her children. For a while, it seemed to Lynette that her life had stabilized. She was able to manage single motherhood and maintain their home. All this changed the week the basement of her house flooded with sewage. Though this was a horrible event in itself, it turned out to be a foreshadowing of darker days to come.

"Honestly, I felt like I was holding it all together very well under the circumstances. You know? Dealing with a sewage flood in a house with two kids. It was horrible, but the cleanup team swooped in to sanitize everything that the flood touched. But that was just the beginning. That same week, my son started developing severe headaches. I thought it must have been related to toxicity of the sewage in the house, so I took him to the doctor. That's when they discovered that he had a brain tumor."

In the days that followed, with the sewage cleanup still happening just beneath their living space, Lynette managed to find the strength and the energy to persevere. She was completely focused on her son's health. She felt that nothing else mattered. Surgery was scheduled. "We talked to specialist after specialist. I prayed. I visualized the tumor shrinking. My son and I said affirmations together: *The tumor is shrinking. It's getting smaller every day.*"

Then, a miracle happened. Preoperative scans showed that the tumor did shrink. What's more, it was determined to be benign. The surgery was deemed unnecessary and was subsequently canceled. Although getting this news should have been the greatest celebration of her life, Lynette fell to pieces. "It's ironic, I know. But in the wake of that relief, it was as if all the trauma I had been holding back to stay strong for myself and my kids. I just couldn't hold it together anymore. It all hit me at once. I went to a very dark place, emotionally. I could barely move. The house just spiraled out of control around me. I was powerless to do anything about it."

Since that day, the clutter took over Lynnette's house. She surrendered; she would simply accept whatever trauma, bad luck, or clutter came her way. She just felt she couldn't fight anymore. She received whatever the

world dropped off at her door. She stopped believing she deserved anything better.

Dr. Green Weighs In on Lynette's Clutter

Lynette's refusal to conquer her clutter following the flood and her son's
illness was her acquiescence to suffering. She subconsciously decided that
if the world intended for her to suffer, that is what she must do. She no
longer felt worthy of happiness. When we feel worthy, we don't mistreat
or deny ourselves. We might punish ourselves by not allowing ourselves
the comfort we so richly deserve. Lynette is denying herself a comfortable home environment by living in so much physical clutter that she
is preventing other people from entering her home. This is a kind of
self-bullying that is so intense it beats any real-life bullies to the punch.
Lynette fears external judgments that she is unworthy of attention or love—
so she uses her home as a way of creating the conditions of rejection. If she
is rejected, she is in control.

Lynette must learn to steep herself in magnificent self-care. She is
worthy by birthright. It does not matter how badly she was treated in the
past; she cannot continue the pattern of self-abuse in the form of self-
judgment. She must set the tone, raise the bar, and offer herself what she
needs. Once she is willing to do this, the Universe will surely follow suit.

Lauren's Decluttering Session with Lynnette

Lynnette and I decide to work on her bathroom. It's unusable. "I usually
just use the kids' bathroom to get ready. I don't enjoy being in here," she
says. And it's no wonder. The bathroom is a wreck. The toilet paper holder
has fallen off the wall. A handle is missing from the sink. Dust has collected around the sink from lack of use.

I tell her, "You need a place of your own to get ready. You are entitled
to some privacy and some 'me' time. You have been so absorbed in caring

for your son that you have forgotten that you must come first. You really can't care for your children unless you are cared for. Being compassionate toward yourself is an act of compassion toward them. If you are constantly self-sacrificing, then you are teaching them that this is what adulthood looks like. If you want them to be fulfilled and self-loving, then you must model it for them."

As we work together to clean out her bathroom, we begin to talk. Lynette is a freelance writer, so I ask her what kinds of things she writes. "Well," she says with a chuckle, "I write profiles for an online dating service. People sign up for this dating service, and if they don't feel like they can make themselves sound good enough, they pay me to write an attractive profile for them."

"So your job is to make someone else look like an appealing romantic partner while you don't feel worthy of one yourself?"

"Yep," she says as she scrubs the sink. "Just a tad ironic, huh?"

"A little," I admit.

As we start going through her bathroom cabinet, I make a discovery. Lynette has tons of expensive makeup: department-store makeup. All in its original packaging, unopened.

I hold it up and give her a look.

"I know. I know," she says with a sigh and a slight smile, "I'm worth it."

In her medicine cabinet, I find two beautiful etched glass bottles with glass stoppers, still sealed. One with body wash in it; the other, lotion. Like the makeup, they are unopened, and they have a layer of dust on them. She explains that they were a thank-you gift from a client that she had done some freelance work for. "I really love the smell of them," she tells me.

"So why haven't you used them?" I ask her.

"They just seem too pretty to use," she says wistfully.

When Lynette breaks the seal on the bottles, something terrible happens. The glass stoppers on the bottles crumble and shards of glass float down into the bottle, making the special liquids inside unusable. It's a sad moment. We're both quiet.

I put my hand on her shoulder. "Listen. Let this be a lesson learned. The next time someone gives you something beautiful like this, use it right away. Don't wait. You deserve beauty and pampering. You are so totally worth it."

Within an hour, the bathroom is sparkling and ready for Lynnette to use. We stand back to take stock of our hard work.

"How do you feel?" I ask her.

"Hopeful," she says. I can tell she means it. "For the first time in years, I actually feel hopeful. Like things can change, starting now."

"Oh, they already have started to change," I reply. "Trust me."

Possible Intention Words for Your Bathroom

Refreshing. Rejuvenating. Reflective. Acceptance. Enjoyment. Ease. Unwinding. Cleansing. Purifying. Energizing. Relaxing. Beauty. Kindness. Compassion.

A Blessing for Your Bathroom

May I find cleansing and renewal in this place. May I find within myself the willingness to accept and love myself, completely. I see that I am aging, but I know that beauty changes over time. I see that there are flaws, but I know that flaws are individual adornments, gems of my uniqueness. I accept myself and embrace my body. In doing so, I accept and embrace Life, for I am its manifestation. May I come to this room daily and see within it the opportunity to experience true love—for Self, Life, and the Divine One who created it all.

An Exercise for Decluttering Your Bathroom

It's time to declutter all the stuff you bought to cover your essential self or run away from your imperfection. It's okay to have creams, lotions, colognes, aftershaves, razors, and tweezers. Goodness knows we all have quite a few. If you purchased those things to treat yourself, fine. Let them stay. But if you went scanning the aisles of the drugstore looking for a product to manage the dimples on your thighs, then that thing must go. If you bought a fancy, expensive razor because you believe your skin is not smooth enough to touch, let it go. If you bought teeth whitening strips because you believe that no one could possibly be enchanted by your natural, beaming smile, then they must go too. We cannot live with evidence of our fears and insecurities. That is clutter that affirms clutter.

Lauren has an insight to share regarding the nature of stray hairs, self-criticism, and self-acceptance to consider as you go about this exercise:

People are not watching you as closely as you think. I can no longer tell when I need to pluck my eyebrows. When I stand face to face with my reflection in the morning, my eyebrows look perfectly fine. If I look in a magnifying mirror, it's another story: I can see lots of little stray eyebrow hairs that my bare eyes overlooked. I used to be pretty scrupulous about plucking out those little buggers as soon as they showed up. Keeping up appearances, you know? Now I walk around for days, even weeks, before I realize they are even there. And guess what? Nobody says a darned thing. Nobody notices. And if they do notice, they don't say anything.

This shows one of two things: either they don't notice and never really have, or that they notice but don't think it's worth mentioning. I mean, honestly. If someone stands up to deliver the eulogy at my funeral and says, "Great gal, but wow, did she ever need to pluck those stray eyebrow hairs," I think that would be more a reflection on them than me, don't you think?

So, what will happen if you stop using that eye cream? What will happen if you have just two colognes instead of ten? Will you be loved or honored less? Or (more likely) will no one even notice? The weird thing is that we are more likely to change our behavior and appearance based on the judgments of people who don't care about us than the people who love us unconditionally. To heck with that, y'all.

Any clutter that speaks to your fears and insecurities gets the boot. Go without it. It's a decluttering exercise and a social experiment. Find out that you can go without, and know true happiness and freedom, which is knowing that you are deeply loved: dimples, wrinkles, stray hairs, and all.

13

....

Your Storage:
Room for Life-Giving Memories

If you want to keep your memories, you first have to live them.

—BOB DYLAN

You can smell the memories before you see them—a heady, familiar mix of cardboard boxes and accumulated dust. It's the smell of faded photographs, dried flowers, and children's drawings on paper that has turned yellow at the edges. This scent has a heaviness that can be felt before we lift a single thing. It carries the weight of years past, of dreams long ago fulfilled or forgotten. You can hear stories being told with peals of laughter or in tears.

Our storage contains pieces of our lives. It can be precious and fragile, oppressive and forbidding. And it can be all of these at once. You might be pulling down the door to your attic, opening a closet, lifting the garage door, or pulling a file drawer in your desk when suddenly the smells, sights, sounds, stories, and emotions you associate with the past come calling. It can be a call that fills your heart with joy or dread. It all depends on how you choose to manage and declutter your storage.

It may be your attic, your basement, or a closet, but we all have a place where we store our memories. There's nothing wrong with hanging on to what's valuable. Trouble is, most of what we put away in the attic is not valuable at all. That's not to say that, at one time or another, it wasn't. But not everything we store away retains its monetary, emotional, or spiritual value. What's more, the more stuff we shove into that space, the less likely it is that we are going to be able to get our hands on the things we need when we want to take them out and look at them.

We hold on to all kinds of stuff: old love letters, clothing that our children outgrew, memorabilia from past vacations, trinkets that we inherited from loved ones. We have lots of reasons to keep these things. They remind us of who we were—of where we come from. It reminds us that time is fleeting.

Yet, our souls are not contained within our stuff. Nor is the meaning of our relationships or the importance of our shared history defined by our belongings.

There is nothing wrong with holding on to our memories. The question is: are our memories framing who we are and giving our lives depth and context, or are they imprisoning us and weighing us down?

The Spiritual Importance of Your Storage

We save things because we are attached to the stories they represent. The words *story* and *storage* share the same root, which means "memory." We have a hard time letting go of clutter that may be attached to our memory of who we once were.

Facing clutter in our storage can be difficult, and it's not just because we don't like cleaning or sorting. We know plenty of people who keep amazingly neat and clean houses who still feel cluttered because what they have stored away is in such disorder.

Our storage has a story to tell. And they are not all easy stories. They include memories of attachments, fears, guilt, regret, disappointment, and worry. We distract ourselves from decluttering the stuff (and these uncomfortable emotions) we have boxed or heaped in our closets, attics, basements, and garages. We put it off. We tell ourselves that we have better things to do. But listen: *there is nothing for you to do that is more important than taking an honest look at the stuff you are carrying around that is causing you unnecessary pain and anxiety.*

When Lauren began to work with people to help them spiritually declutter, she noticed that when a client knew there was something in their storage they needed to let go of—and felt highly ambivalent about releasing it—they made a particular face, which she calls "the Splinter Face." First, the client would hug the object close to their heart and hold their hands over it protectively. When Lauren empathized with their attachment to the object but confirmed that it was time to let go, the client grimaced and sucked in air through their exposed teeth.

For a while Lauren wondered, *When have I seen people make that face before?* It seemed so familiar. Then she remembered: it was the face her children used to make when they showed her a splinter that needed to be removed. Lauren would put on her glasses, lean in closely, and say, "Okay, we need to take that sucker out." And they would react by hiding their hand against their chests, grimacing and slowly sucking air through their teeth. Their actions show

how they anticipated the pain of having the splinter removed. But in reality, the anticipation was much worse than the removal itself. The removal turned out to be a relief—and so much better than having something festering under the surface that was actually causing pain. The decluttering clients had the same reaction at the prospect of having their clutter removed.

It's natural to feel ambivalent about removing clutter. Like a splinter, we know that the clutter is not part of us. It has become emotionally lodged under our skin, so removing it *feels* like we are removing a piece of ourselves. Clutter is not part of your essential self, but you have to breach the boundaries of yourself to remove it. You have to get past some history, some emotions, and some fears, all of which (though not the essential self) are closely identified with the essential self. If you identify with your clutter in an unhealthy way and imagine it is part of who you are, it will—like a splinter that we are afraid to remove—start creating pain that is very real.

Your possessions are not *you*. If all of your possessions were to vanish, you would still be you. You would still be whole. You would still have a history. You would still love what you love. You would still be beloved by the Universe, a spark of the Divine. You know that, right? You are loved for simply being you. You were manifested into this world to be precisely who you are. By letting go of the clutter you are storing, you are not removing a part of yourself. You are, in fact, removing what is not you, so who you are can shine more clearly, with vibrant health.

You came into this world with nothing. You'll leave with nothing. In the period in between, you will amass possessions and stories and emotions around your possessions. Some of these possessions, emotions, and stories serve you, while others do not. But none of it—you hear us?—is actually *you*.

It is easy to say "release everything that does not serve you: possessions, obligations, relationships, roles." The trouble is that so many people don't know who they are. We don't know what serves us. We confuse who we are with possessions, obligations, relationships, and roles—stuff. You are none of those things. You are a unique manifestation of the Divine in this world, a light revealed just once in creation. Your stuff either serves that or gets in the way. Declutter what's blocking your light.

Decluttering Grief and Making Room for Memory: Joanne's Story

When Joanne meets me at the door, it is with a warm smile and a joyous embrace. Being in Joanne's presence gives me the feeling of being special—like I belong. It's a quality she shared with her husband, Dave.

Dave was the love of Joanne's life. She met him after her second marriage crumbled. Joanne's adult daughter had already moved out of her home. So, from the time their lives first came together, it was just Joanne and Dave. They had one another, and frankly that was all they needed. They were business partners, best friends, and soul mates.

All that ended one night about six months before I came to Joanne's house. Dave arrived home late from chorus practice. As was her habit, she called down the stairs to ask him how it went. "Just fine!" he replied. Those were the last words she heard from him. Just seconds later, Dave collapsed from a massive heart attack. He was rushed to the hospital, but he never regained consciousness. A few days later, surrounded by friends and loved ones, he passed away quietly.

When Joanne speaks of Dave, she wavers between a broad smile and tears. She is alternately warmed by his memory and crushed by his absence. She feels like she is bumping around inside her home—a home they created together. Sometimes, she feels completely at ease. She feels Dave's presence and she is comforted by it. But there are also moments when the enormity of her loss crushes her and she feels terribly alone.

When Joanne reaches out to me to help her declutter her home, I ask her up front if she is interested in sorting through Dave's belongings. I acknowledge that her grief is still fresh, and wonder if she is ready to look at his things.

When we sit at her dining room table, I ask her this question again. She pauses and breathes in deeply. "Every day I go into the walk-in closet that the two of us shared. Half of it is his. Half of it is mine. I honestly don't mind getting rid of about ninety percent of his stuff. He only wore a few things anyway. It's not the getting rid of it that bothers me. It's just that . . ." Her eyes well up with tears. She takes a deep, shuddering breath. "It's just that if I do that, his half of the closet will be empty. And that, I don't think I can bear."

I reach across the table to take her hand. I am crying too.

Dr. Green Weighs In on Joanne's Grief

Grief is a process. It can't be rushed. It can't be pushed. It takes its time. Sometimes it goes below the surface for hours, days, months, and even years, only to resurface anew. As long as grief keeps moving and flowing, it is a healthy process of letting go. On *Hoarders*, I see frequent examples of people who are locked into a complicated, unprocessed grief—a grief so strong, and which the client identifies with so greatly, that they cannot separate themselves from it. They have become their grief and everything they do is acting out of that grief.

This is not the case with Joanne. For Joanne, this grief is new. It is natural for it to come and go as it does. She should not try to push her grief away, even if it seems to come at "inconvenient" times or take her by surprise. This is a healthy and necessary process of letting go.

Joanne should not force herself to part with Dave's memory. It's very dear to her. She spent the best years of her life with him, so there is no timeline for letting his memory go. This is a time for her to be with her feelings and acknowledge their depth. Right now, her love dwells where her grief dwells. They are intermingled. Sometimes she will feel nothing but love, easy and uncomplicated. At other times, she will find grief in her heart. And that's all perfectly okay.

As Joanne goes about decluttering, she needs to be aware that grief may arise. She needs to take care of herself and not try to move too quickly. This is a time for honoring Dave's memory and their love together.

At the same time, if she is too afraid to spend time in that place—if she is too afraid of touching or moving his things—her grief may get stuck. Touching Dave's things and becoming familiar with the feelings they bring up is the best way for her to process her grief.

Lauren Helps Joanne Declutter the Office She Shared with Dave

It is clearly too soon for Joanne to move anything out of Dave's half of the closet. At the same time, she doesn't want to leave things just as they were on the day he passed away. After a tour of her home, we settle on their shared home office. She shows me Dave's desk, where his files sit in tall stacks, just as he left them. We finally settle on a bookcase that belonged to Dave. It not only has books in it, but some random office supplies as well: binder clips, a stapler, a little framed photo of a child. "I don't even know who that child *is*," Joanne chuckles.

There are also several upright containers of magazines. "I know he meant to get to those," she says. "And I know I am not going to ever read them." She reaches out to remove them, but I stop her. Rather than take things off the shelf that she doesn't want to keep, I suggest that she first remove the things she knows that Dave loved. The books that really meant something to him and that stir her heart in his direction.

"That's the opposite of what I've been taught," she replies.

"Well, it's important that you hold and embrace the things that mean something to you before you remove them. Let's set them aside as sacred. Then we'll make room for them on the shelf. And you can replace them exactly as you wish."

This is precisely what Joanne does. It is a profound experience for her. She is able to touch Dave's memory by touching what he loved. She is able to discern between those books he truly loved and those that meant very little to him. By removing what he loved from the shelf first, then clearing away the reading he didn't care for, and finally replacing his favorites, she feels his memory. She experiences his presence even more powerfully. The added benefit is that decluttering yields enough room for her to place a few favorite, framed photographs of Dave on top of the shelf.

In the process, Joanne learns that by letting go of some of Dave's possessions with gentleness, compassion, and mindfulness (as well as an awareness of her own grieving process) she is inviting his memory to come through even more clearly, and she feels his presence shining even more brightly, which is a great source of comfort to her.

When we are done, we step back and look at the work we accomplished together. We stand silently, side by side, and I put my arm around her shoulder. Joanne once again begins to tear up, but this time she has a smile on her face. "That was powerful. And I truly feel hopeful."

I am sure that is precisely what Dave would have wanted.

Possible Intention Words for Your Storage

Useful. Organized. Life-giving. Life-affirming. Treasured. Comforting. Light. Free. Compassionate. Easy. Open. Spacious. Enjoyable. Ease. Helpful. Supportive. Special.

A Blessing for Your Storage

May I have the wisdom to only store what is meaningful, helpful, and serves the life I am living. May this room not represent fear of letting go but willingness to shift and change with time. May I have the wisdom to realize that even though I may treasure what is in here, it is not me. It has never been me. It may tell my story, but I am the living essence of that story. May this place be open and free. May it only hold what I truly treasure and need, and may I have the courage to let go of what I do not treasure or need. May the thought of this place make me feel peaceful and safe. May I always be a wise steward of its contents.

An Exercise for Decluttering Your Storage

All the possessions you have in your life are like foreign objects in the body—which is to say they are not part of your essential self. That is not to say your stuff is all bad. Some possessions can help you serve the world as you were intended to—like a pin that is implanted to hold a bone together. Your stuff may be a "foreign object," but it can be essential for you to move freely. Others, like those pesky splinters, are preventing your freedom and enjoyment of your environment. You are not taking anything away from yourself by removing the splinter. You are actually enhancing your life and your power to do good in the world.

This is your affirmation for decluttering objects that are painful to let go of:

This object has found its way into my home and my life, but it is not me. It is preventing me from living fully and happily. It is stealing my power. It is preventing me from caring for myself, communicating with others, and getting me where I need to go in life. I don't care how much it hurts to remove it. I am going to do this so I can get back to the business of being me and serving the world.

14

....

Your Breathing Room:
Room for Mindfulness
and Compassion

We have a room for everything—eating, sleeping, watching TV—
but we have no room for mindfulness. I recommend that we
set up a small room in our homes and call it a breathing room,
where we can be alone and practice just breathing and smiling,
at least in difficult moments.

—THICH NHAT HANH

A room for mindfulness, compassion, and forgiveness. For peace and reconciliation—and nothing but those things. Can you imagine a room that would take a higher priority than this? Is there anything more important than cultivating peace in this world that is so frequently torn asunder by violence and anger? By creating breathing room in our homes and hearts, we not only have a compassionate refuge, we become a compassionate refuge. And there is perhaps no greater human calling than becoming a compassionate refuge for a world in need.

So many times throughout the day, we find ourselves squeezed into painful, claustrophobic spaces in the heart. We might be feeling angry, frustrated, demoralized, or fearful. And it doesn't take a major incident to trigger these emotions in us: a child balancing too many plates while clearing the table trips and shatters the whole stack; we're checking out at the grocery and realize we've left our money at home; we're stuck in traffic and the person behind us feels the traffic might move faster if they lean on their horn. Regardless of what pushes us into these difficult emotional states, when they press in on us, we feel like we have no choice but to act out of our anguish. So we yell at the child and all too late realize that we've brought them to tears. We call ourselves all kinds of cruel names for having left our wallet at home on the kitchen counter. We angrily offer our middle finger to the horn-honker behind us. And we genuinely feel in that moment that we have no choice in the matter.

But what if it could be different? What if you had a place you could go to in order to find comfort, compassion, and consolation in moments such as these? Remember for a moment what it was like to be a child in pain. Perhaps you had fallen down and scraped your knee. Perhaps your best friend shunned you on the playground. Maybe despite your best efforts, you failed a test. In that moment of pain, you wanted to hide or to run away. Or maybe you simply wanted to lash out and scream. If you were fortunate, you had a parent or a grandparent or a teacher who would take you up in their arms and suddenly you would feel all the tension, grief, and fear wash away from your body. And in the quiet that followed, you heard the beating of their heart. Your breath slowed to a steady rhythm. And you knew that everything was going to be okay.

We have the capacity to offer ourselves this same kind of comfort and consolation in our homes and hearts by creating breathing room within them. Your breathing room is a place where you can go for this kind of essential compassion that is necessary to transform your difficult emotions. It is a place where you can feel the loving embrace of compassion, where all your fears and anger can be released, and you can return to feeling your breath, the simplest reminder of the miraculous nature of your being.

There are times when we lose track of the sheer wonder of life and we become locked into patterns of pain that are unnecessary. We don't have to be pushed and pulled by our difficult emotions. We are essentially larger than any of these emotional states, but we must find breathing room to know that remarkable fact. Mindfulness and serenity are the way, for inner and outer peace. There is no greater gift you can give yourself but the gift of wide-open, compassionate space. It's time to declutter and make that room. When we find a way to open up a place in our homes that is dedicated to compassion— whether that is a whole room or even a chair that sits in our home precisely for these moments when we are feeling caught—we give ourselves a gift beyond measure.

When we create breathing room in the home, we prioritize peace. When we prioritize peace, we create breathing room in the heart. And that breathing room is a grace we can create for ourselves and the world. It is a gift to self and a grace beyond measure.

Releasing Internal Clutter and Creating Breathing Room: Angela's Story

Angela is young and brimming with energy. She is a yoga instructor and massage therapist by trade. When she speaks of the spiritual life that is at the core of her life's journey, she breaks into uncontrollable giggles, as if the energy of joy can't possibly be suppressed.

When Angela greets me at the door to her home, her face breaks into a broad smile and she begins to bounce on the tips of her toes like a little girl whose best friend has just arrived for a play date. Her wild tangle of black curls bounces along with her, as if the energy of her unbridled spirit can't be contained or tamed. She throws her arms around me. "I am so glad you are here," she says. She steps back, folds her hands over her heart, and bows her head, smiling. When she lifts her eyes to me, they sparkle with life. This is a young woman who is spiritual to her core.

When offered the chance to declutter her living space using spiritual principles, Angela jumped at the chance. As both a spiritual healer and a teacher of movement, she understands very keenly how the physical, emotional, and spiritual aspects of our selves are intertwined.

She is in her midtwenties and just starting her healing practice in a new city; like many young people, she does not have an apartment of her own, but rents a room in a shared house. Stopping in the kitchen to make me a cup of green tea, she says hello to some of her roommates, a couple of young men with beards who nod an absent hello to us.

We grab our tea and retreat to her room, which consists of a small closet, a chest of drawers, and a mattress that sits on the floor. Strung from the ceiling is a string of white Christmas lights that sweetly twinkle in the dimmed room. She shuts the door quietly and the two of us sit down on her bed with our tea.

She smiles at me and I smile back—I can't help myself. Her smile is absolutely infectious. But I am beginning to wonder where the clutter is. She did tell me she was cluttered, but this room is about as simple and pared down as a life gets. When I mention this, she reminds me about the yogic principle of *aparigraha*—not owning more than you need. She tells me a story about her great-grandmother who passed away, leaving rooms and rooms full of expensive clothes. Her great-grandmother's hoarding was a source of stress to her family in the wake of her passing.

"Just thinking about all that stuff makes me itchy all over. It makes me want to crawl out of my skin." Nonetheless, Angela came away with several pieces of treasured clothing from her great-grandmother, who was quite a fashionista. "We happen to be the same size!" She beams. "Isn't that amazing?"

Angela switches gears to tell me a story about something that happened to her just that day. She had arrived home from work to find a letter addressed to her on the counter. In the envelope was a check for one hundred dollars, with a note from an old friend: "The Universe told me to send this to you."

During the course of our conversation, Angela tells me several stories about the Universe supplying her with just what she needed, precisely at the moments when she thought she was bereft and without support. I begin to notice a trend.

I say, "So I notice that you are very fortunate in that the Universe is able to give you what you need just when you need it. But I'm wondering . . ."

The smile vanishes from Angela's face. I lean in to let her know that I feel enormous compassion for her and am not judging her at all. "I am wondering if you feel you are capable of meeting your own needs when you need it."

Angela's tears begin to flow. She reveals to me that she was abused as a child. "There's a lot of pain. A lot of unworthiness," she says.

Dr. Green Weighs In on Angela's Clutter

Even though Angela lives with virtually no physical clutter, she has a suffocating amount of internal clutter. So even if she can stretch out her arms in her room to spin around and dance, she now needs to find that same expansive space inside herself. She may have plenty of breathing room in her living space, but emotionally and spiritually—where it counts—she has no room to breathe.

Angela has pared down her life so dramatically that she doesn't feel comfortable. The more cluttered we are (whether physically or emotionally), the more unworthy we feel. We all have strands of unworthiness that we are trying to untangle in order to unfold and become our true selves.

Angela feels she is unworthy of deep, rich comfort, so she is denying herself these things before the Universe can. She is hiding behind spiritual principles in order to own her poverty and say, "I meant to do that." If she is poor, it is because she intended it. She is in control of the poverty, so she doesn't have to feel rejected, should the Universe deny her riches.

Spirituality is not about self-denial, it is about self-enlargement. It is about connecting the Higher Self with the ego self, and seeing that the ego self is a part of the Higher Self and a manifestation of the Higher Self, the way every wave is part of the ocean, but at the same time, made of nothing but ocean. The principle of *aparigraha* is intended to reduce our possessions in order to see through to that larger truth. It is not meant to make us feel small and impoverished. It enables us to see our greater spiritual riches.

Angela is a victim of child abuse and it makes sense that someone who is suffering in such a way would want to be small, diminished, or unnoticed. Angela must practice declaring her largeness. She must claim her inner breathing room and expand into it. Ultimately, she will come to learn that she is truly safe in the expansive embrace of the Divine.

Lauren Helps Angela Declutter

Angela wipes away her tears. We sit in silence together for a few minutes. I want her to simply know that I am present to her pain and her fear.

She looks up at the twinkly holiday lights that hang above her bed. "I use these for light because I won't buy myself the lamp I really want." It turns out that she does want a lamp. And a rug. And a bed with a headboard. She wants comfort, ease, and warmth.

I suggest something to Angela that I don't typically recommend to clutterers: splurge on yourself. Angela lives with a different kind of clutter than the piles of boxes and clothes some people hang on to. She has the hidden clutter of unworthiness that is common in people who are victims of child abuse. I recommend that she invest in herself and treat herself as she wants to be treated. She can't wait on the Universe to provide her with the beauty her soul desires. She must affirm her soul's desire herself.

The emptiness of her room is not breathing room. It is suffocating. In a very real way, it is not empty at all—it is filled with the clutter of fear and suffering. In order to find true breathing room, Angela has to make this room comfortable. She needs and deserves a place where her ego's fears can release, where she can truly relax, let go, and feel deep and abiding compassion for herself.

Three weeks later, I run into Angela at a concert. She can barely contain her excitement. "Lauren! You're going to be so proud of me! I bought myself a lamp. And a rug. My room feels so warm and cozy. Things are changing. They're shifting. I can feel it. And the best part is: I am the one who is making it happen."

Miracles happen when we allow ourselves comfort and compassion. When we allow ourselves breathing room.

STEP THREE

clear the energy

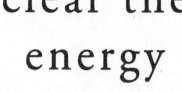

15

....

The Ten Principles of
Spiritual Decluttering

Now that you have set your intentions for each of the rooms in your home and your heart, it is time to start clearing away the clutter that does not belong. These principles are meant to be implemented holistically across every aspect of your life, not just your physical home.

Each of these ten principles has four exercises that accompany it to help you declutter your heart, home, relationships, roles, and responsibilities. As you know, clutter can build up in any one of these aspects and begin to influence the others. For example: if you carry too much clutter in your heart, you will find that you are manifesting that clutter in your home. Then, if your home is buckling under the weight of clutter, you might find that your relationships are suffering—your clutter consumes so much physical, mental, and emotional energy. If your relationships are cluttered with consuming emotions, you will find that your time is consumed by relationships that drain you. And then, if you have taken on too many roles and responsibilities, your time is perpetually short, and your energy is drained by consuming emotions like resentment, guilt, and bitterness, you will be carrying emotional clutter—which leads to physical clutter, which can cause your relationships to be cluttered. It's all interrelated. All clutter affects you spiritually, whether it's home clutter, heart clutter, time clutter, or relationship clutter. It blocks your essential Divine light and your ability to touch the world with that light.

As you read through the principles detailed in this section, you will probably find that some speak to where you are in your life more than others. For example, perhaps you would like to feel more gratitude in your life, and Principle #3, Letting Go with Grace and Gratitude, speaks to your heart. We suggest that you do all four exercises in that section so that you can experience the holistic impact of this principle across every level of your life. Remember that it is important to declutter on every level in order to make room for the Divine light to shine through. The more you are able to release, the more freedom you will experience.

Let's dive in.

16

Principle 1:
Don't Attack—
Clear with Compassion

When we hear people talk about clearing their clutter, the most frequently used word we hear is the word *attack*, as in "I am going to set aside this weekend and attack the clutter on my desk." To this, we answer: Stop! Don't attack anything!

You are not in a fight with your clutter. It is not your enemy. It is not evil. It only holds as much energy as you are willing to give it. When we say we are going to attack our clutter, we are saying that our clutter is powerful, and we need to gird ourselves for battle. *Our clutter has power over us to the degree we give it power.* If we treat it like a strong adversary, we are going to wear ourselves out before we've even begun.

Decluttering does not have to be a fight. Here's the thing about fights: they require adrenaline and they utilize our animal brain. Whenever we engage our adrenaline, we cannot process deeply or think clearly. We cannot use our higher-order reasoning skills, access our real emotions, or feel our connection to the Divine. In order to be our most loving, wisest selves, we need to be able to access all of these. As we do this important spiritual work, we don't need to be ruthless. We don't need to be heartless.

The other thing we need to remember about adrenaline is that our bodies produce it when we are under stress. Adrenaline causes a surge in energy that can be very powerful—while it lasts, that is. But the energy of adrenaline is quickly depleted. And then what happens? We are exhausted. Our brains go numb. Our limbs go limp. We can't move another muscle. We appraise the work we've done and think how hard it was, how little we accomplished despite the energy we spent.

So we need to clear with compassion. For ourselves, yes, but also for our clutter. Rather than thinking of clutter as an enemy that needs to be vanquished, we are going to think of it as a small, lost child who wandered into the wrong place. We can treat it with gentle curiosity ("Now, how did you get in here?"), quiet honesty ("You don't belong here."), and ultimately a firm hand ("C'mon. Let's get you out of here and back where you belong.").

We must remember that we know best. We set the intention and decide if it is being met. If we are going to get the job done, we need to clear with an energy that is sustainable for the long term, so we can return again and again without becoming exhausted or depleted. This is work that requires your best self, so you need your best energy to accomplish it. You need the energy of compassion.

Decluttering Your Home with Compassion

Imagine being a small child and wandering off from your parents, following a blowing leaf or tracking your own shadow on a sunny day. Suddenly, you look up and realize that you are in a sea of strangers. A face appears out of the crowd, and seeing your fear, crouches down to your level. The stranger asks, "Are you lost?" You nod your head, not yet knowing if this is a person you can trust. Perhaps this person flags down a police officer or a clerk at the store, letting an authority know that you are lost. But that person does not leave you while you wait for your parents. They smile gently to you the whole time, never losing confidence. They project happiness and assurance. Their smile says it all: I will not leave you until you are back where you belong.

This is the same sense of compassion that we must have for our clutter. You are the helpful adult to the wandering child. You are solid, kind, friendly, and trustworthy. Your task is to guide this wanderer safely back to where it belongs.

Right now, we are just going to work on the clutter that needs to be moved to another room or needs to be donated so that it can serve someone else. Get two boxes or bags: one marked "relocate" and one marked "donate."

Always begin by setting your intention for the room or the area that you are clearing. You are going to look for things that do not resonate with your intention and that need to be put into one of your boxes. You're looking for things that either belong somewhere else in your home, in a space with a clear intention or they do not fit with any intention in your home and are better off with someone else.

Now, picking up each object, draw into your heart the compassion you'd feel for a lost child. To some of these objects you'll say, "You have wandered into the wrong room. I know just where you belong." Those objects go in the relocate container. To other objects, you'll need to say, "You have wandered way too far. My home is not the place for you at all, but I am sure we can find somewhere you do belong." Those objects go into the donate container.

We need a different kind of compassion for things that have served their purpose, do not belong in your home, and cannot be donated. These items simply need to be thrown out. That can be the hardest thing to do. When we throw things out, we can feel that we're being wasteful and ungrateful.

How is it possible to throw things out with love? It would seem that throwing things out is the opposite of compassion. Think about a party you have at your home. Your most conscientious guests have already left. But there's a group of folks that just won't go. They're living it up, and they couldn't care less about how you feel. They don't care how tired you are or how much energy you've already given them. So what do you do? Do you push them out aggressively? No, they'd just push back, dig in their heels, call you names, and demand another drink.

Here's what you do: sidle on up to them and say, "Oh my gosh! You all are still here. You must be looking for your coats. Here! I already have them for you. No, don't worry, I'll help you put it on. Here's the door. No, you don't have to stay to help clean up. You've done enough already just by being here. You've honored me with your presence. Now be safe out there, okay?"

And you shut the door. You can hear their laughter on the sidewalk. They're happy, not offended. You offered them compassion. They needed a hand and a direction to go, and you offered it.

It's hard to throw people out of your house, just like it's hard to throw objects out. It might feel as if you are dishonoring them and their intentions or being inconsiderate and ungrateful. But you're not a bad person—not at all. You are honoring the sanctity of your home and your need to rest easily within it.

Decluttering Your Heart with Compassion

When it comes to decluttering, it's important to recognize that compassion is an action. It is not passive. You can't just let things stay the way they always have been. When we feel compassion for a person who is suffering, we are not stuck there. True compassion is the desire for suffering to transform into relief, and ultimately into joy.

Wallowing in suffering is not compassion; that is self-pity. Self-pity implies a passive observation of our pain, one that does not wish to transform pain because it is strongly identified with it. Self-pity is a kind of negative self-talk that you must declutter.

For the next few weeks, pay attention to the negative self-talk that is harming your spirit. We are so unconscious of the messages we feed ourselves daily that we can fail to realize how toxic our inner environment has become. We internalize these hateful messages so frequently and so unconsciously that we don't realize the damage it's doing to our hearts and souls. It is as if we are slowly ingesting poison without even recognizing what it is; we are the ones making ourselves sick.

For this exercise you will need your decluttering notebook.

Whenever you have a negative thought about yourself, write it down. Now, this is not about pitying yourself for having self-pitying thoughts. This is not about thinking, *Look how many terrible things I think about myself. No wonder I feel so bad. I am a hopeless self-abuser!* That is just one more self-abusing thought. Instead, we're seeking compassion and transformation. For every negative thought you have about yourself, you are going to write an equally powerful positive affirmation of your blessings and a vow of action to affirm the blessing and honor it.

It's important to recognize that most of our negative thoughts and complaints have to do with blessings that we are not taking full advantage of in life. Make sure that the vow of action is doable. For example, if your vow is about eating healthier food, you may want to vow to eat a healthy breakfast tomorrow instead of vowing to lose fifty pounds. Remember, this is about compassion: taking on vows that are burdensome is likely to lead to more self-affliction.

Here's an example. You record the self-pitying thought: *My home is a wreck.* Your accompanying affirmation of blessing might be: *I am blessed with a home,* and *I vow to remove ten things today to help reveal the blessing of my home.*

Maybe your negative thought is: *I am completely unreliable. I am constantly letting my friends down.* In that case, your accompanying affirmation of blessing could be: *I am so blessed with friends. Today I am going to call a friend, make a date to see her, and hold that time sacred.*

One of the reasons we want you to write down your negative thoughts is to be aware of how many you have during the day. You may be surprised at how many uncompassionate, negative things you tell yourself. By writing them down—externalizing them—you are breaking your habit of subconsciously internalizing them. You have to be willing to take a look at the thoughts you carry around and examine the many ways that you abuse and disempower yourself with your own thoughts.

There is one additional compassionate decluttering step in this exercise. At each day's end, tear your negative thoughts out of your notebook and release them. Take the pages out of your home, to the trash or recycling—the compassionate thing is to remove them completely from your home.

Tear these thoughts up and say these words, or something similar: "I release these negative thoughts that are unkind to my heart and my spirit. They have burdened me terribly, but now they have no weight or substance. These thoughts have been trying to push me toward becoming a better person, but all that they have done is disempower me. They are misguided. So I release them with compassion, so that I may affirm my blessings with full compassion for myself and those around me."

Now, go back into your home and pick up your notebook. You are left with the blessings in your life and your vows of action to affirm those blessings. Breathe deeply as you read these blessings. Read them again and again, until you are really able to feel and embody them. Then follow up on your vow. Be a person who is able to release negativity with compassion, affirm your blessings, and take action to make your blessings vibrantly real.

Decluttering Your Relationships with Compassion

Not every relationship serves your spirit or the way you want to show up in the world. Deeply compassionate, our souls often want to serve others with no consideration of how those people may be draining our energy or making it impossible for us to be compassionate toward Self.

In the previous exercise, we explored the notion that compassion should not be confused for pity. Wanting the best for someone is very different than feeling sorry for them. But we often keep people around in our lives because we feel that they will be hurt if we release them. We worry that, without us, they will be bereft—this belief is at the root of all codependent relationships. So no matter how much their behavior drains us, hurts us, or annoys us, we believe that the compassionate thing to do is to let them, for as long as they please.

You get where we are going with this, right?

To allow someone in your life who is a constant source of negativity shows an extreme lack of compassion for yourself. That could not be clearer—we hope. But here's some more food for thought: you're not being compassionate toward the negative person by allowing him to believe that his consistently hurtful behavior—deliberate or not—is in service to his spirit. Allowing this person to stay in your life, with no boundaries or consequences whatsoever, gives him the false, dangerous impression that he's fine. Your choice communicates that the path he is currently walking—a path that cuts directly through his heart—is the right path for him.

But it isn't. You are absolutely empowered to blow your traffic whistle and hold up your hand, letting him know that his path stops at you. If he is unwilling to change his behavior, he must turn in another direction. He may go where he pleases, toward either pain or liberation. (Let's hope it's the latter.) Simply put, allowing him to continue to hurt you is not a path that serves either of you.

So here's the straight scoop about decluttering your relationships with compassion. You need to get very clear (with yourself and the other person) about what is not working for you. There is a chance that this person may be motivated to change his behavior. If this is the case, he is making a very important affirmation. It means that his relationship with you is more valuable than his habits, and that he is willing to sacrifice and make changes in order to keep you in his life. That is a fantastic outcome! What a gift to know that someone is willing to give up his old ways in order to continue to be part of your life.

The opposite may be true as well. He may simply decide that his habits are more important than his relationship with you. He may have found that the only thing he enjoyed about your relationship was the fact that you—consciously or unconsciously—supported his habits. We're really sorry, if that's the case. It's hurtful to know that someone would choose old habits over you or use you as a means to keep engaging in a particular habit or behavior. Maybe you have been avoiding this conversation because you know, deep down, that when push comes to shove, this person will put his habit first. Maybe you don't want to deal with that reality.

Ultimately, it is more important to seek clarity now than to go on for years and years avoiding a conversation. This writing exercise is going to help you understand how to deal with the people in your life whose behavior is lacking in compassion toward you.

Take out your journal so you can answer the following questions. They will help you pull together what you need to say to these negative people. As you do this exercise, you may want to bring a specific person to mind.

Ask: What energies are you currently trying to invite into your life—love, compassion, joy, peace, relaxation? Why do you value this person in your life? What positive qualities does he offer? How does he support you? What specific actions has this person consistently taken that obstruct these energies in your life (such as calling late at night to complain about coworkers, asking for your advice but not taking it, making a mess of things and expecting you to pick up the pieces, or telling you why your dreams are foolish or why your best ideas won't work)? What role might you have played in allowing this person to think it was okay to do this? How can you let this person know that you value who he is and what he brings into your life? How can this person support you as you clear the way for positive energy to manifest in your life?

If you truly value this person, you'll need to find the courage to relate this information to him. We know it's not easy, but if you want to keep this person in your life, you must. It's the compassionate thing to do. The journey of compassion is not always the easy path to walk; it leads through the desert of suffering before it opens to the oasis of happiness.

You might also be thinking, *I just realized that I don't want to offer this person the chance to stay in my life. I happen to know that he values his habits over my companionship. I am quite certain that his relationship with me is entirely about feeding his habit.*

In that case, you know just what you need to do: declutter that relationship. You can still relay your feelings, but let this person know that you're done. It's compassionate to yourself. Eventually, he may realize the errors of his ways and be motivated to change. Withdrawing your friendship may give him the motivation he needs to change.

The bottom line is this: every person who walks this earth has a path to tread. Not every path goes through your home and heart. Be clear about that, and you'll be on the path to freedom.

Here's the extra, added benefit: once you are clear about what you want, you will no longer waste time on relationships that are unfulfilling and draining. When someone new shows up at your door, you'll know right away if he is the kind of person you want to welcome. So you'll either throw open the door and let him in or you'll say, "No, thanks. I'm not buying what you're selling," and then gently shut him out. He will move on. No harm done.

Decluttering Your Roles, Obligations, and Schedules with Compassion

Many of us spend our time running from one end of the day to the other, barely leaving ourselves the opportunity to breathe. We know from our work with clients that this behavior more often than not results in exhaustion, depression, anger, frustration, and resentment.

Dr. Green notes that in her practice, most of her clients are burned out and exhausted because they are not living in their own authentic truth, which makes them depressed and anxious. These people tend to come in telling the story that they are exhausted because their schedules are too busy, too full. This is undoubtedly true. It is also the case that these people are keeping themselves busy because they are afraid of encountering their authentic selves. There is an inherent drive to avoid the mystery of the human experience. It's not that there are no opportunities for rest and silence. It's that we are afraid of what we might encounter in that silence. We fear the unknown. So we keep ourselves busy and distracted with stories that we do know and are familiar with.

If we change, we will likely encounter pain, but we might also find freedom—but only if we are willing to find the room to breathe.

If you are a person who says yes to every activity, project, social engagement, and volunteer opportunity, you may feel you are being a compassionate, thoughtful person, always caring for others—but in fact, you are probably also feeling like a martyr, drained, exhausted, and resentful. If we are compassionate toward others without offering compassion toward ourselves, overwhelm will be the result. Giving more than you receive sets you up to run at a deficit. It won't be long before you suffer burnout. That's not compassionate to you, to the world, or to others.

Perhaps you have heard of the 80/20 rule in volunteer organizations? The 80/20 rule posits that 20 percent of volunteers do 80 percent of the work. This is clearly an imbalanced, dysfunctional model. Believe me, the 20 percent have plenty to say about how hard they work and how the organization would fall apart if they didn't. But has the 20 percent ever stepped back? Have they committed an act of trust and allowed anyone else to step in? Probably not. If you are in the 20 percent that does 80 percent of the work, it may be for a few reasons:

- You don't have faith in others
- You have a high need for control
- You are worried that things are going to fall apart if you step back (or out)
- You are in the habit of complaining about not getting enough recognition for how hard you work

Try this: say *no*. Give yourself a rest and enjoy taking it easy. Have a little faith. Step back. Wait. Allow someone else to step in, and let them make their mistakes. Give others an opportunity to shine. You are building a world in which faith, trust, and self-care are fundamental. You are rejecting a world where burnout and resentment fester under the surface of organizations whose mission is compassion.

17

Principle 2:
Out with Consuming Emotions, In with Sustainable Emotions

For the purpose of this book, we are going to classify emotions into two simple categories: *consuming* and *sustaining*. In the natural world, we look at resources as consumable or sustainable. Consumable resources are depleted faster than they can be regenerated, if they can be regenerated at all. Over time, the demand for more resources cannot be met—we just run out. Sustainable resources, on the other hand, have the capacity to regenerate just as fast or faster than we are able to use them. These resources can be maintained or become more plentiful.

Our emotions are the same. We pour ourselves into some emotions, but they give us no energy in return. These are the consuming emotions we talked about earlier. These emotions do not make us into better people, connect us with people we love, yield wisdom or insight, or draw us closer to the Divine. But they *do* solidify our sense of ego, further our suffering, and increase the illusion of our separation from one another and from our Divine Source. If we look around our houses, we will find evidence of these consuming emotions everywhere we look. If we harbor them in our hearts, it is highly likely that they are manifesting physically in our homes.

Sustainable emotions are just the opposite of consuming emotions. They enliven us. They melt away ego and the need to be right. They make us feel vital, drawing us closer to our fellow human beings and to our Divine Source. Want to know if an emotion is sustainable? Try putting it into this sentence:

**"In his heart he felt a deep sense of _____
    and he knew that everything was going to be all right."**

These words fit perfectly: *happiness, compassion, love, joy, trust, faith.* For one thing, they all take our ego out of the picture. When we experience sustainable feelings, we know everything is going to be all right because their source is not the ego. They are not limited by the ego's limitations. Every ounce of energy that we pour into creating these energies in ourselves and in the world pays us back with even more of the same. When we invest our energy into sustainable emotions, we are sharing them with the people who live in and visit our homes. When our homes are truly decluttered, we are making room for these energies to flow, unobstructed.

What causes the obstruction of sustainable emotions? Consuming emotions. Our goal in decluttering is to be vigilant about the arrival of these consuming emotions and their physical manifestations. We can't let them linger. We need to claim ample room for the light of our sustainable emotions, as well as room for their joyful physical presence in our belongings.

Releasing Consuming Emotions in Your Home

This is a sorting exercise unlike any you have tried before. Rather than sorting things into "give away" and "throw away" piles, you are going to sort them according to the emotions they bring up in you.

Get four pieces of paper. On each one, write the name of a consuming emotion: worry, guilt, regret, fear. (There are more than just those four, but let's start there.)

When you pick up an object, hold it to your heart. Your heart chakra is a sensitive energy center, which allows you to feel the energy of the object. You might like to practice with something you truly love and treasure. Pick up that valentine with the handprint on it that your child made for you or the quilt that your great-grandmother sewed for you. Hold that treasured object and really feel the flow of that sustainable energy to your heart. If you close your eyes and tune in, you will be able to feel it flowing—the energy of love, happiness, and kindness. You will feel uplifted and strengthened.

Not every object is going to do this for you, though. In fact, objects that carry negative energy will make you feel drained when you bring them near your heart. You may feel a twinge. You may feel a wrench. You may feel a terrified fluttering, akin to a trapped animal. You may feel a subtle sickness. You may feel a sinking sensation.

Once you have these sensations through your heart center, you are onto something. Look at the four pieces of paper you have laid out on the floor. Which pile does this item belong to? Once you let go of it, commit to letting it go for good. There is absolutely no need for you to keep any of these emotions lying around your home. They are draining you and your environment of your precious energy.

Just how much of your stuff are you hanging on to because of guilt, regret, worry, and fear? It is important to have an awareness of how much physical and emotional space these specific emotions take up in your life. If we are to work toward decluttering these emotions, we must first take stock of how much power they have over us.

Now remove those items. Donate, recycle, or trash them. It's up to you—but you must commit to getting rid of the consuming emotions that are eating up your life energy!

Releasing Consuming Emotions from Your Heart

If there is one thing in this book we feel that you absolutely must do, it is this: learn how to recognize the seeds of consuming emotions in your heart and stop watering them.

Every heart has within it the seeds of every emotion—both sustainable and consuming emotions. The interesting and ironic part of this is that the seeds of our positive/sustainable emotions require much more care than our consuming emotions, which seem to grow without much mindful attention at all. In a garden, weeds don't need much encouragement to grow. All they need is a little sunshine and water to take over, consuming the precious mineral resources that your flowers and vegetables need to thrive.

Our hearts are the same way. Our consuming emotions don't require careful cultivation. They crop up on their own and occupy our hearts very quickly. Most of us have, from time to time, poured a lot of fertilizer (ahem!) on them to encourage their growth. We can become quite proud of the weeds in our hearts. Look how tall my resentment has grown! Look how my bitterness has taken over this small bed inside me! See how my depression is spreading out, touching everything! We can get so ensnared in our weeds that we forget that the entire reason to have a garden is to cultivate beauty and nourishment.

Any good gardener will tell you that it is impossible to have a garden that is free of weeds. By the same token, there is no such thing as a heart that is free of consuming emotions. The goal of having a decluttered home is not to make clutter disappear forever. Of course clutter shows up! But once we've decluttered, it's easy to see when it shows up again. We can identify it and take care of it quickly. Gardeners will tell you the same thing about weeds. You should learn what they look like and train yourself to see the difference between your weeds and your cultivated plants. Don't wait until they are so tall that they eat up the sunlight that is meant to feed your beautiful blossoms.

You must learn to do the same for your consuming emotions. Learn to see your bitterness at the moment it first appears. Train yourself to see your sadness before it becomes depression and runs rampant. Eradicate it at the roots. Know its source and what feeds it. At the same time, give the flowers of your sustainable emotions what they need to flourish: the rich soil of self-care, the light of Divine presence, the waters of compassion, and lots and lots of fresh air and breathing room.

Now, take a moment to reflect: How do you know when consuming emotions are beginning to take root in your heart? Complete these sentences:

- I know the seeds of (bitterness, guilt, worry, resentment, envy, fear, and so forth) are taking root in me when _____.
- I feel these sensations inside my body: _____.
- I hear myself thinking these kinds of thoughts: _____.

Just a hint and a word to the wise: you will probably feel the sensations in your body before the thoughts register in your mind. You must slow down and become quiet within your mind and your body, so you can tune in to these subtle thoughts and feelings. It is essential to create breathing room in our lives so we can achieve this kind of subtle yet deep tuning-in.

Once you become practiced at subtle noticing, you won't have to wait until your garden is choked with consuming emotions. Don't water them. Just treat them as you would a weed in your garden: a simple acknowledgment, followed by an intentional and gentle removal. Then, you can turn your attention to the sustainable emotions you want to nurture and grow.

Releasing Consuming Emotions within our Relationships

There are relationships built on consuming emotions. And the sad thing is, we feel that these emotions reflect the relationship bond's health. Some people come to equate worry with love. These people think: *If I love you, I want your safety above all things, and so I worry about you.* They rely upon guilt and worry as expressions of love. They feel that the bonds created by these two particular emotions make a relationship strong and keep it safe from harm; it is a strange, twisted outcropping of love.

One woman we spoke to while writing this book, reflecting on her relationship with her adult daughter, told us, "She doesn't worry about anything, so I think she really appreciates that I worry for her."

To which Lauren asked, "Have you ever confirmed with her that she appreciates you worrying? Have you ever asked her if that is her experience?"

"No," the woman said, raising an eyebrow. "Why wouldn't she?" Later in the conversation, she laughed that she and her daughter have an unspoken bond because "we feel guilty about the same things."

In reality, love creates emotional safety. Compassion creates emotional safety. Trust and faith create emotional safety. We must invest those emotions in our relationships if we want our loved ones to return to our embrace again and again.

Guilt shows an essential lack of trust in the relationship. It does not strengthen the bonds of the relationship; it actually drives people away. When a person is on the receiving end of a guilt trip in a relationship, they are being told: *I don't really trust your love, so I need for you to prove it.* For example, if a person says, "If you don't call me, you must not love me," they are telling the other person that they don't trust the bond of love they share. They need a phone call to confirm that love is alive and well.

Viewed this way, it is easy to see that underneath guilt is the fear that the love isn't real or isn't strong enough. The person is saying, in essence, "I am worried that I have not done enough to earn your love, so I need to implant guilt within you so you are motivated to prove to me that you *do*." There is a very close bond between lack of trust, fear of losing love, worry, and guilt. None of this is a healthy form of emotional bonding. In fact, it can indicate that someone in the relationship probably had an insecure bond with a parent when they were young.

This can manifest in the home when gifts are given and people are afraid to remove these things, even when they are no longer of service to the home. If there is a bond of guilt or worry in the relationship, we hear people say, "If my mother finds out I gave this away, she'll be crushed," or "My daughter will feel I don't love her or support her if I throw this away." We even had a client whose mother-in-law would come to visit, bring gifts for the grandchildren, and tell them, "Now, you can't ever give this away." Can't you just see the fear and the worry in the poor grandmother—the fear that she is unloved and easily forgotten? Can't you just imagine the children's confusion and the fury the daughter-in-law might feel? Where love is concerned, our unchecked insecurity becomes worry, which becomes guilt, which cascades into confusion and rage. Even though love is the underlying message, it cannot be heard over the din of consuming emotions.

Worry and guilt have no place in our most loving and trusting relationships. If you have a guilt gifter in your life, you don't help them by hanging on to the object of guilt. It strengthens the illusion that the gift is the proof of their love; keeping it becomes proof that you return the sentiment. This illusion is only causing suffering for both of you.

If you are the guilt gifter, you must understand that guilt is not the tie that binds you to people you love. Love is that bond. Trust that. Anyone who gives away a gift from you is not disposing of your love. (How could such a thing be possible? Love is infinite and eternal and so could never be parceled out and disposed of or destroyed.) Any gift you offer (whether it is fresh from the department store or a family heirloom) must be given without attachment or not at all, because guilt is no gift. Worry is not an expression of love.

Guilt gifting is just one example of the way consuming emotions manifest in our relationships. There are many other consuming emotions that might tie us to the people we love: mutual resentments, common fears, shared hatreds. None of these are healthy forms of bonding. If we let these go and find that the only things connecting us are consuming emotions, then perhaps there is no relationship to save. But if we let go of these consuming emotions, we will very likely find that there is a deeper bond based on love, respect, and understanding. In order to find this, we must learn to let go of the false bond of consuming emotions.

Decluttering Your Roles, Obligations, and Schedules of Consuming Emotions

The difference between people who rise in the morning with hope in their hearts and those who face each day with dread may have more to do with the emotions they experience during their daily activities than the activities themselves. It's not the activities that drain us, but our attitude toward what we do and the emotions we carry while we do those activities that drain us of our precious energy.

Take for example, two people working side by side on a Sunday afternoon, loading up cans at a local food pantry. One person has chosen this to be the one, special volunteer activity he does each month. He looks forward to it. He knows the people who will be there are fed by the energy of the activity, nourished in mind and spirit. He is completely present, in the moment, feeling positive about the impact he has in the community. He is practically bubbling over with energy. He quickly fills each box, and while he does, he attempts to connect with the other volunteers working near him by sharing how much this work means to him.

The person next to him, however, is dragging. She was asked to come here by a coworker and she felt guilty about saying no. She was worried that saying no would make her look like a person who does not care about others, or like someone who's insensitive about the suffering of hungry people in her community. And her coworker didn't even show up! In fact, a quick look at her smartphone confirms that the coworker is having a picnic by the river. She is fuming. The guilt and worry that she felt is replaced by regret and resentment. And on top of it, there is some annoying guy standing next to her, with a huge grin on his stupid face, talking about how he does this every month and how good it feels. She'd tell him that she has five other organizations she volunteers for already, but she doesn't want to seem like she's bragging. All she wants to do is go home and crawl back into bed. The day has just started and it already feels like a huge waste.

At the end of this volunteer shift, which of the two do you think is going to leave feeling energized? Who will go home and have a meaningful conversation with their family? Who will bring the sustainable energies of happiness, love, and encouragement back into their home?

The difference between these two people is that one person is motivated for all the right reasons. His motivation carries him through the activity and out the other side. The second person is motivated by consuming emotions, so she becomes more and more consumed as she goes. And that is just how it works: both sustainable and consuming emotions create a cascade of similar emotions. Love generates happiness, while guilt generates anxiety. Sustainable emotions take people in an upward spiral, while consuming emotions take people in a downward spiral.

Sometimes the emotional clutter we carry into our homes is the result of our activities and roles outside of the house. If we want to be at our best at home, we need to manifest our best energy when we are out in the world. Of course, our homes are meant to be refuges, and they should be deliberately designed and maintained as "safe zones." But if we believe that our home is a safe zone and the world is a jungle, then home is not actually a refuge—it is a hideout. Somewhere in our consciousness, even while we are in our homes, we will have anxiety about life outside our door.

For this exercise, take out your journal and go through all the various roles, obligations, and elective activities you participate in. Fill out the following chart, and be honest about what emotions come up. First, divide your page into three columns. Write the following headings at the top of your three columns:

Role/ Responsibility	What motivated me to become involved	How I feel when I complete this task, role, etc.

We want you to consider letting go of roles that are draining you. It doesn't have to be a loss. Remember that by stepping aside, you will be making room for someone else to take your place—and he or she might actually enjoy it more than you. Don't assume that because you no longer enjoy one of your roles, responsibilities, or activities, that no one possibly could.

We need to create breathing room in our schedules so that the activities we choose have the potential to nourish us. If we are constantly operating at an energy deficit, even the things we should enjoy—including being at home, in the company of people we love—can become a drain.

18

······························

Principle 3:
Letting Go with Grace
and Gratitude

For many of us, being a spiritual person means living fully in the moment with grace and gratitude. It means acknowledging the blessing of life as a gift generously given and eventually taken. The great spiritual masters of every tradition have tried to help us live with the reality and inevitability of death so that we might embrace life fully while we are here and not waste our time on petty pursuits. To know that life is impermanent does not have to be a cause for fear or depression. Instead, it should inspire deep gratitude for every moment.

There is a truth we all must face: a time will come when we must let go of this life in order to become one with Eternal Life. If we live well, we will be able to let go with grace and with gratitude, in full awareness of the opportunity we have been given to love, offer compassion, and fully realize the spark of Divinity we enjoyed in this lifetime.

So as we live, we must practice letting go with grace and gratitude. This is perhaps the deepest aspect of spiritual decluttering. It is our opportunity to practice letting go—to say, *This has served me and now I release it as a blessing.* We could also say the opposite: *This does not serve me, so I relinquish all attachment to what has caused me or others to suffer.* Clinging to life will do us no good. The belief that we own life is an illusion. We say "my life," but no spiritual tradition has ever affirmed that any of our lives actually belong to us. Clinging causes pain, and release liberates us from that. The goal of decluttering, spiritually speaking, is liberation. Everything we relinquish is a small act of liberation that will help us become comfortable with the great freedom that will ultimately come to all of us.

Letting go does not have to be painful. It can be an act of grace, a living gratitude. May we each look within as we declutter our homes and hearts to release what does not serve us. And may we do so with a smile and a thank you, not just for the thing itself, but for the lesson it teaches us. May we feel gratitude for the opportunity to draw closer to our Source, and ultimately for the practice of letting go of ego and attachment—the deepest spiritual lesson we can encounter. And wonder of wonders, we can do this in the safe and loving comfort of our very own homes.

Decluttering Your Home with Grace and Gratitude

Just as we want to feel gratitude for those things that we truly love, embrace, and want to keep in our lives, it's important to say thank you to the things we need to let go of. If they never really served us at all or did nothing but drain us of our energy and cause pain in our lives, then we need to forgive them and let them go.

One of the reasons we give ourselves grief over letting go of clutter is that we feel we are ungrateful for those objects. This exercise is a cure for that particular kind of guilt. We also have trouble letting go when something we bought, inherited, or received as a gift never fulfilled its purpose, and we want to keep it around until it does. So rather than keeping it around (and letting it sap our time and energy), we need to forgive the thing for not being what we had hoped it would.

This exercise is just a simple conversation to have in your heart. You might also benefit from working aloud, if using your voice helps you deeply feel it. All you need to do is to pick up the object and speak to it as if it were your friend. Imagine, for example, an old pair of jeans. You enjoyed them for many years, but they have become too threadbare to wear any longer. Say to them, "Thank you for being there for me. I had so much fun wearing you. You were so comfortable and I have so many great memories attached to you. But now, I can't wear you out in public anymore. It doesn't mean I don't love you. I'll always carry that memory in my heart."

Now you are probably thinking, *I will feel very silly talking to a pair of pants*. All right. We get it. But is it any sillier to hang on to a pair of torn jeans because you have nice memories of them? Your pants are not people, but you are having feelings about them as if they were. Why not just be honest in your heart and have a kind, compassionate conversation with them? This doesn't have to be out loud. (You don't need your children walking by your bedroom and wondering why the heck you are talking to your jeans!) The conversation and the expression of gratitude might be exactly what you need to let them go.

And as for the things in your life that never really served their purpose? Let's think of that frame your mother-in-law bought with a nonstandard photo size—you know, that frame that wound up in the "guilt pile" in one of the previous section's exercises? The one you held to your heart and suddenly got that sinking, nauseated, heavy feeling of oppressive guilt? It's time to forgive that frame. You may say, "Okay, frame, you showed up in my life as a gift. I really hoped that I could find a photo to put in you, but it never happened. It's not because I didn't try. I did. But there are just no photos that fit in you. I forgive you for not being what I had hoped you would be. I forgive myself for needing to let you go. In this moment, I feel nothing but forgiveness for the past, and all I hoped would be but never was." Forgive the frame. Bless it. And then let it go. Take it to the donation drop-off center, where someone will see it and scream with glee, "Oh my gosh, I have been looking all over for a frame this size!"

It's important to practice gratitude and forgiveness in this way. Gratitude and forgiveness are not only spiritual principles, they are spiritual practices. Like all practices, we need to do them over and over to get good at them. To be a grateful and forgiving person in this world is to be a shining standard of humanity. If we practice now, offering small gratitudes and forgivenesses for the little things we need to let go of, we will find the heart to offer large gratitudes and large forgivenesses for the big things.

We do this to practice grace, courage, and dignity. When the time comes for the big letting-go, we want to be full of gratitude for what life has offered us. We will have forgiven what life has not offered us. Until then, we learn not only how to let go of life, but how to embrace it while it is here.

Decluttering Your Heart with Grace and Gratitude

Our homes become cluttered when we hang on to objects for longer than they are useful to us. They stopped serving us ages ago, but we just can't seem to make ourselves give them up. Ironically, it's often our gratitude for the object that makes us unwilling to release it. For example, imagine you have a sweater that you loved several years ago. It was so warm and soft, your go-to item on chilly days. You felt cozy as soon as you pulled it over your head. But then, you accidentally threw it in the hot water wash with your whites and it came out two sizes too small. The sweater is now itchy, and so small you can barely get it over your head. The sleeves want to crawl up above your wrists and the neck suffocates you. When you wear it, you feel slightly claustrophobic. You keep picking it up and wishing it was different, but it's not. Now you can't seem to let it go, even though it can't serve its original purpose of keeping you warm on a cold day. It's your gratitude for what the sweater did for you in the past that makes it hard to let go.

Like a shrunken sweater, there are certain emotions that we hang on to because they once served us, but they no longer fit who we are now. Perhaps they once provided us with a sense of safety, but over time, they've come to limit our emotional range, suffocating our happiness.

There may have been a time in your life that you needed to protect yourself from a person or a situation that felt threatening to your spirit. Perhaps you loved someone, trusted that she cared for you, gave yourself over fully to her care, and then found out that your trust was grossly misplaced. By opening your heart to this person and allowing love to flow in without obstruction, you opened your life to a world of pain. In response, you did what is natural: you closed down. The portal of your heart became a small, cramped space like a cocoon: safe, ideal for you to develop in, and far away from the threats of the world.

But there comes a time when every butterfly must spread its wings. The cocoon is no longer of service; in fact, it endangers the next phase in the metamorphosis. A butterfly that cannot free itself from its cocoon is in danger of losing its life.

So just as we must bid a fond farewell to the sweater that is too small, and the butterfly must say goodbye to its cocoon, so you must thank the defense mechanisms that kept you safe in an emotional crisis. You can understand that this response no longer fits you and is endangering your free movement and flight.

Each of us needs to look within ourselves for those tight places—hardheartedness, suspicion, cynicism—all those defense mechanisms that kept us safe when we were still tender from being hurt. Now we can see them for what they are: temporary shelters from the elements of life that might have hurt us. We need to come to rely once again on our inner strength, not our outer defenses.

To our hardheartedness we must say: "I realize that you came into my life to protect me from emotional injury. You were afraid that anything could happen at any time. You thought the only way to shield me from further injury was to protect me completely. I want to thank you for protecting me. I feel strong enough to allow love to touch my heart again. I release you from your role as sentry so I can open again. I give you gratitude for your service."

To our suspicion we must say: "I know that you look at everyone as a potential criminal—and me as the potential victim—but I am tired of viewing the world this way. Being on constant alert is exhausting. I don't want to suspect that everyone in my life is out to get me. I want to trust again, and you are preventing me from doing that. So I want to thank you for helping keep people at bay while I healed. I am stronger now, and I would like to judge people based on my experience, instead of fear. I gratefully release you from your protective role."

To our cynicism we must say: "I had such beautiful expectations of life, and my expectations brought on disappointments. Each disappointment made me feel like I was crashing to the ground. You told me: 'Expect to be disappointed and you'll no longer be hurt. Be prepared and you can't be injured.' I no longer want to live like this. I believe that I am better off taking the risk of occasional disappointment than remaining closed off. So thank you for trying to help me. I no longer need your counsel."

We must declutter our hearts of these protectors in order to live fully. We need to trust our heart's native strength and wisdom. Hardheartedness, suspicion, and cynicism can shield us for a while in the wake of emotional injury, but in the long run, they do more damage than good. Declutter them.

Decluttering Your Relationships with Grace and Gratitude

Just as we outgrow clothing that has become too small, we outgrow relationships.

After you make a decision to grow in your life, you might notice some close relationships that just don't fit or suit you. Perhaps you have friends whose belief systems are so different from yours that you find you have very little in common. Perhaps you have friends whose biting cynicism was once funny, but you now find grating—or just downright depressing. Maybe there are people in your life who simply cannot accept those whose race, religion, or sexual orientation is different from theirs. Perhaps you have people in your life who can't understand the direction your life is taking. Maybe they have fears about where you are going, so they either try to hold you back with their doubts or outright undermine your efforts. People like this are probably not going to improve the quality of your life as you grow in heart and spirit.

We want you to understand that you can love people without keeping them close to you. If you have to steel yourself to be in their company, you are making a dangerous trade: you are trading vital, life-changing energy in order to maintain a toxic friendship. You are sacrificing who you are in order to allow this friend to maintain their idea of who you were in the past. Pretending to be what we are not in order to fulfill an image that someone else has of us does not serve us or them.

It's important to be clear with the people in your life. Let them know who you are, where you stand, and where you are going with your life. There is no point in pretending in order to spare people pain; ultimately, pretending (and living a lie) creates more pain than it prevents.

We have a fear of being mercenary if we leave others behind. We have the impression that this is a unilateral choice: we are charging forward and our friends or family are left to eat our dust. But parting ways is their choice as much as it is yours. It is a mutual decision, even if they do not acknowledge their part. The decision to stay rooted in place is still a decision. Grow forward and give others the opportunity to come with you. If they choose to stay rooted where they are, you cannot stay with them. Have a heart full of gratitude for the path you have traveled thus far. Hug the people you've outgrown, thank them, and continue gracefully down your path. Move confidently and courageously. There may be a chance that when they see your confidence, courage, and, ultimately, your freedom and joy, they may be inspired to follow your example.

This would be a good time to take out your decluttering journal to write about gratitude. This exercise is meant to reveal the full history of your relationship with another. It is intended to help you understand that outgrowing this relationship does not make you a bad or ungrateful person. In your journal, write:

- The name of this person
- How you came to know him
- What first drew you to him
- The positive qualities you first saw in him
- How you grew as a person by having him in your life
- The many ways you have grown since

You can also draw a diagram showing how your paths came together, what you experienced walking side-by-side in life with this person, and how your paths diverged.

Below your diagram, write a simple note of gratitude for this relationship and what it offered to you, using the words and imagery from your journal. Take a few moments to let this sink in. If you feel the need to speak to this person about your feelings or about your need to step back from the relationship, you will be able to proceed with courage, grounded in love and gratitude.

Decluttering Our Roles and Responsibilities with Grace and Gratitude

Here's your mantra. Are you ready? It's pretty simple, and it goes like this:

Thank you for the opportunity to serve.

Got it? Good. Because you are going to need it. Starting now.

When it comes to collecting roles and responsibilities in life, our schedules get cluttered in the same way that our houses do. You bring things in and nothing goes out. There is a mathematical logic to clutter: if you take in more than you let go, your house is going to become an overburdened, draining mess. This is true for your schedule as well. Say yes to everything and you will quickly find yourself in a big heap of overwhelm and exhaustion.

Here's the good news, and it also depends on mathematical logic: you can easily maintain a healthy schedule, as long as you let go of one responsibility for every new responsibility you take on. Period. So whatever you take on, you must love it more or find it more fulfilling than at least one other thing you are already doing.

We understand: you have lots of passions and interests. Lots of people depend on you and look up to you. You don't want to disappoint anyone (least of all yourself). But you are one person and you have only so much time in each day. So be selective.

Whenever you are offered a chance at a new opportunity, get out your mantra because you are going to need it. Say it twice—once for the responsibility you are taking on, and once for the obligation you let go of.

To the new responsibility, you are going to say: "Thank you for the opportunity to serve. I appreciate the chance. I will continue to do this task as long as it is mutually beneficial." Why mutually beneficial? Because it is not just about being of service to the person or organization; it's about finding work that is beneficial to your own personal growth. You can benefit by learning real skills, in relationship, in heart, or in spirit. When the responsibility reaches the point that it is serving them but not you, let it go. Be clear on this. With the exception of parenting, no role is guaranteed forever. Period.

To the obligation you need to let go of, say, "Thank you for the opportunity to serve. I am so grateful to have been a part of this, but it is time for me to move on. I feel good about making room for someone else to step in. I wish nothing but blessings for your future."

Carry your mantra in your pocket. If you are a person who is energetic, valuable, and trustworthy, you will need to use it a lot. Being asked to take on these responsibilities speaks volumes about the person you are. Take it as a compliment. The more valuable you are, the more you'll need your mantra.

Don't be afraid to use it.

19

....

Principle 4:
Accept Where You Are

Believe it or not, your path to enlightenment starts in your clutter. Yes, right in the middle of the pile of clothes you never wear, those unmatched Tupperware items, that stack of mail you need to sort through, and the cabinet full of hotel soaps and shampoos that you've been stashing away for years. That is where your path to freedom begins. Isn't that exciting? You start right where you are. This is a process that happens little by little—every unnecessary object you remove draws you closer to liberty. Think of each piece of clutter as a stepping-stone on the path to freedom.

To begin decluttering, we must first accept where we are. Stand amid the chaos and say to yourself, "Okay. This is where I am." Your habits of being and acquiring have brought you to this place and this moment. Denying where you are will only get you more of the same. The Buddha taught that running from pain, denying it, or pushing it away creates suffering. Your clutter is a result of running away from your pain. Your habit of denying that there is a problem causes the problem to grow. The only way out is through. So the first step in decluttering is knowing that we want freedom, peace, and ease—and affirming that we are worthy of these gifts.

If you tell yourself, "It has always been this way and it will always be this way," then you are living with mental clutter. But by simply removing that one thought, you have taken your first step on the path. You have already begun to declutter.

Decluttering Your Home with Acceptance

We are big fans of before-and-after photos. It's delightful to look at where you once were so you can see how far you have come. Progress is easy to forget. The mind has a remarkable way of looking at how things are in the present and saying, "This is the way it's always been."

Lauren has noticed that even if she has worked for a couple hours on decluttering a space, her clients are blown away when they see "before" photos. They have already forgotten what the room looked like when they started.

Here's the other thing about Lauren's decluttering clients: all of them—and we mean *all* of them—ask Lauren if they can clean up before she gets there! They want to present a clean front. Unfortunately, this is part of the cluttering problem. We want to hide our clutter, from others and ourselves. We can feel a lot of shame and overwhelm when we are in a cluttered space. We want to get away or tell ourselves, "I'll deal with this later." But those are not options for you anymore. Honestly, there is no moment but this moment. Therefore, we recommend that you take pictures of your mess just as it is. These photos are a record of where you were when you started to declutter, as well as a way of showing yourself where you are now.

Take your camera or your phone to the space you want to declutter and simply stand within it. Breathe. Your first step is simply to do this: feel your feet on the floor and your breath going in and out of your lungs. Stand there until you no longer feel the need to run. Then, say these words:

"This is where I am. This is my clutter. I accept that I created this. The chaos and the indecision in my life has cluttered this place with my inner chaos and indecision. I accept this. There is no shame in this. I release all shame. There is no guilt in this. I release all guilt."

Look around you and allow yourself to experience peace. This is simply where you stand. There is no right or wrong about it. No judgment. It simply is what it is. Smile. Breathe. Know that with full acceptance, your life has the opportunity to change. You can only move forward from where you stand. You will accomplish this with courage and compassion as your faithful companions.

Now pick up your camera. This is a kind of commitment ceremony to yourself. You are going to look through the viewfinder with your finger on the button and you are going to say this to yourself and mean it:

"The moment I press this button is the moment my life begins to change. From this moment, I vow to remove what no longer serves me and create the energy that does. I will no longer simply accept what life throws at me by default. I will choose what makes me feel healthy, whole, and alive."

Now press the button. *Click.* That's it. Now you have a record of the moment that your life began to change as well as proof of your vow. You have accepted who and where you are with compassion. Now, you will move forward.

Decluttering Your Heart with Acceptance

Whether you are decluttering your home or your heart, you must start where you are—there is no other place to start.

You are afraid? This is where you begin.

You are brokenhearted? This is where you begin.

You are overwhelmed and confused? This is where you begin.

We propose trying something radical: love where you are right now, no matter how hard that place is. Love your difficulty. Love your pain. Love your fear, broken-heartedness, overwhelm, and confusion. Loving it doesn't mean you want things to stay the way they are. On the contrary, love your life because you want it to change. Love is the only power in the world that can transform it. Love acts in faith in what is not seen: light within the darkness, meaning with the chaos. Love is essentially courageous because it is willing to go into the darkness to redeem the light. It is willing to venture into the chaos to rescue meaning. Martin Luther King Jr. said, "Darkness cannot drive out darkness; only light can do that. Hate cannot drive out hate; only love can do that." Love is the ultimate transformative power. Loving what's lovable is easy. Loving what is difficult to love—that is the transformative work of life.

If you are in a difficult place, the only thing that can change your situation is love and acceptance. You cannot change it by pushing it away, denying it, running from it, or excusing it—you can change it only by loving it, being present to it, and showing a steady, open-hearted willingness to see things through.

We must be able to look at the emotions we don't like—such as fear, broken-heartedness, and overwhelm—acknowledge them, accept them, and even love them as we send them on their way to transformation.

There is no emotion that cannot be transformed by your solid, stable, courageous, and willing presence.

Decluttering Your Relationships with Acceptance

We must accept people for who and where they are in their lives. This is the only way to have honest and fulfilling relationships. We must be able to see them and ourselves fully, with openhearted clarity.

If an aspect of a relationship isn't working for us emotionally, we owe it to ourselves and the people we love and honor to take an honest look at what is not working and why. Here, we are talking about love and honor in the spiritual sense, not just the emotional sense. We can love people without liking their behavior; we can honor their humanity without respecting their choices.

There are two kinds of acceptance, and it is very important to distinguish between them when we are decluttering.

One kind of acceptance says, "This is the way it is, so this is the way it always will be." This kind of acceptance is delusional. Nothing in life is immutable. To accept in this way is to give in to unhappiness.

The other kind of acceptance says, "This is where I am now, so this is the starting point for change." This kind of honest acceptance and ownership of our emotions is necessary for all healthy relationships. And this acceptance begins with self-acceptance. You must be the one willing to accept where you are. You must be willing to state that with full honesty.

When we begin to tell people that we are looking for change, we must first let them know that we love and honor them as human beings. However, we should be careful to never use the word *but* to express where we are. The word *but* implies that what you said about love and honor is either not true or not as important as your request for change. We are all in the habit of saying things like, "I love you, *but* you need to do a better job of cleaning up after yourself when you cook."

Instead, try saying this, "I love you and because I love you I don't want anger and frustration to get in the way of that love. I have been frustrated at the state of the kitchen after you are done cooking." This is all honest and true. Also, notice that the word *you* is not mentioned. These are statements about yourself, who just so happens to be the only person you can take responsibility for in the relationship. You are expressing your own feelings and accepting responsibility for transformation. That is where true heart decluttering begins.

Decluttering Your Roles and Responsibilities with Acceptance

When we are feeling overwhelmed by our roles and responsibilities, we often express our pain by casting blame for our feelings onto the other party. We blame our overwhelm on others' expectations of us, never questioning whether that expectation is true—or whether we had a part in setting up that expectation.

Lauren has a funny story to tell about that:

When our four children were small, I left my job to be with them full time at home. My husband worked outside the home. When he walked in the door every night, the house was clean, the children were bathed, and dinner was on the stove—so he could relax. Every day, I felt like I was in a race against time, trying to get everything perfectly in order for him when he walked in the door. It was extremely stressful.

So one particularly stressful day, he came home and I let him have it: "I just can't do this anymore! I work all day trying to keep up with the house and entertain the kids. I am exhausted. You walk in and expect everything to be just perfect, so that you can unwind and relax. Well, what about my relaxation, huh? Does it seem fair to you that I have to wear myself out making everything perfect for you—that I have to be a stressed-out mess just so you can unwind?! Does it?!"

My husband stood and stared in disbelief at me, a wild-eyed, resentful woman that he barely seemed to recognize. He shook his head like he was trying to shake off an unpleasant hallucination. "Hold on," he said, putting up his hand. "When did I ever say that? I never said I expected all that work to be done by the time I came home. I would be perfectly happy to help cook, bathe the kids, or both. I like doing those things. I just never do them because they are done before I get home."

Oh.

I learned my lesson. I was creating my own stress because I had created unkind expectations based on an assumption about what my husband wanted. It turned out that the opposite was true. I never asked the question, "What would you like to do?"

Before we assume that other people have unkind and unfair expectations, we need to ask ourselves, "Did they actually expect me to do this? Or am I taking it on with the assumption that this is what they expect of me?"

Sometimes, the easiest way to declutter our work responsibilities is to declutter our own unkind expectations of ourselves. We can remove the idea that other people are to blame for our stress when we create those conditions ourselves.

Accept responsibility. Stop pointing fingers. Ease up on your expectations of yourself. It's a simple way to declutter your time.

20

Principle 5:
Just Say No to Clutter Enablers and Clutter Dumps

In life, we tend to attract the same the energy we put out. This is why miserable people swear up and down that humanity is miserable, and why happy people say that in their experience, most everyone they meet is happy. When people are miserable, grumpy, cynical, or misanthropic, they see that mirrored back at them. It takes a very strong person not to fall under the shadow of negative energy, so a person who is chronically unhappy or disappointed influences others around her to be just the same. Soon, everyone she meets is unhappy or angry. Her experience affirms her assumption: people are generally unhappy, greedy, insincere, and can't be trusted.

The person who is happy and hopeful has a similar experience. People around him are affected by his demeanor. They smile in his presence. They reflect back his light. They want to connect whenever possible and share their positive experiences with him. From his perspective, people are, for the most part, lovely; they are kind and helpful and good and happy. His experience also affirms his assumption: people are generally happy, kind, warm, and helpful.

So what does this phenomenon have to do with clutter? Clutter attracts clutter. Cluttered people tend to attract clutter into their lives.

For a moment, picture in your mind's eye a room that is beautifully simplified and decluttered. It is open, filled with light, and shining with positive energy. Now, imagine that someone comes in and tosses a coat in the middle of the floor. It is glaringly obvious that the garment is out of place. It will quickly be whisked away and either put back in its proper place or taken out of the home. It has the same effect as saying something cynical to a person who is happy. It won't stay in the room for that long, because it just doesn't have a natural place to rest.

Now picture a cluttered room with papers on the floor, clothes piled up, unfinished projects in the corners, and unpaid bills on the table. Imagine that someone dumps a bag of clothing in the middle of the floor. It just disappears into the clutter that is already there. It doesn't make much of a difference. The room just absorbs it. In the same way, if you dump loads of negativity onto someone who is cynical, she will just absorb it.

Clutter masks clutter. Clutter hides clutter. Clutter camouflages clutter.

So it is no wonder that when people want to clean out their closets or their basements and unburden themselves of their clutter, who do they tend to dump it on? *You.* People leave their clutter with clutterers. Just as a person who has cynical thoughts and negative feelings to unburden will unload their negativity on a cynic, people who have clutter to get rid of will bring it a person who will absorb their clutter. Unfortunately, if you are cluttered, that person is you.

The people who dump on you usually feel that it will not make a difference, because you are already cluttered. But it does make a difference—a huge one. Whether it's emotional or physical clutter, you do not need to be a dumping ground.

So if you are cluttered, you probably have at least one clutter enabler in your life: your sweet old aunt, a solicitous neighbor, a "helpful" coworker. The enabler is a person who shows up at your door with a big black trash bag and a smile on her face and says, "I just did a huge spring cleaning and found all of these clothes that don't fit me. I thought maybe you'd want them." You, being the accommodating person you are—or maybe the fearful person who is afraid to turn away anything free!—grab the bag without even thinking. You don't put away its contents where they belong—no way. You toss the bag in the corner with the other kind donations, into the morass of clutter.

Don't blame the enabler. She feels like she's just walked into a win-win situation. She wants to get rid of her stuff by giving it to someone who will value and appreciate it. She knows you will take it with a smile. The trouble is, she has not brought you more happiness; she has increased your burden.

You need to learn to say no to the clutter enablers in your life.

Declutter Your Home by Saying No to Clutter Dumps

It isn't easy to say no, especially to gifts from people you love, people who want to help you, and people who want the best for you. If you happen to be a clutterer, you may have a harder time saying no than most people. Clutterers are often kind to a fault. And you know what? Your enablers know that, which is one of the reasons they bring their unwanted stuff to your door. They happen to know that other folks (non-clutterers) will say no thanks, so they don't even ask. They come right to you.

The first thing you need to do is to identify your enablers. You may have one or several. For this exercise, you are going to use your journal to complete the sentences below. This will help you get clear about who your clutter enablers are and how they affect your life. The choices below are just suggestions: you may have a very different set of feelings and reactions. You should include your most honest assessment as you write:

_____ is a clutter enabler in my life.

This person brings clutter into my house _____.
    a) frequently
    b) occasionally

This has been happening for _____.
    a) weeks
    b) months
    c) years

When this person brings items to my door, I feel _____.
    a) delighted
    b) guilty
    c) uncomfortable
    d) burdened
    e) exasperated

f) grateful

g) other _____

Up until now I have felt _____.
    a) that I have to take it because I might need it at some point
    b) fearful that I would appear ungrateful to say no
    c) that I don't have the right to say no to any gift
    d) that I would hurt this person's feelings if I say no
    e) worried that if I don't take it, it will go to waste
    f) other _____

I am now committing to saying no to this enabler in my life
because _____.
    a) I can't take on any more clutter in my home
    b) I need to change the dynamic between this person and
       myself
    c) I want this person to see me as more than a receptacle for
       unwanted things
    d) I need this person to support me in becoming uncluttered
    e) other _____

Using your answers, write a speech to this person. You don't need
to include everything you wrote in your journal. Most of it is just to
help you get clear on your own feelings. When the clutter enabler
comes to your door or calls to say she is coming over with a carload
of stuff (or even a couple of bags), we want you to be prepared.

Your speech might go something like this:

Hi, _____. For the past
_____ you've been bringing things

from your home over to my home. Though I really appreciate what you've done for me, I want you to know that I am in the process of decluttering my home, so I really can't take anything new or donated. I have been concerned about telling you because I don't want you to think I am ungrateful. That is not the case. Right now, I need all my friends and family, including you, to support me in removing things from my home. I truly thank you for everything you have given me in the past, but from here on out, I just can't accept what you are offering.

You may be wondering: What if I do want what the enabler is offering me? What if I could use it? Let us ask you these questions in response: Did you know what was in the bag before they called? Did you need it before they called? Why do you think you need it now? If you didn't need it five minutes before the phone rang—or before they showed up at the door unannounced—then you don't need it five minutes after. Period.

If you are going to change this relationship, don't just change it by degrees—change it completely. If this person supports you completely, then she should understand. Will she get it right away? Perhaps not. Will she try again because she doesn't quite believe you mean it? Probably. But you must be firm and consistent. You are trying to change the relationship. If you had a problem with alcohol and one of your old drinking buddies offered you a drink, it might be hard for that person to understand your decision.

When you change your habits, you are asking the people around you to change as well. Over time, they will get it or move on. If you have a clutter enabler who needs you to feel happy and grateful for their clutter, and their self-esteem is based on you accepting their gifts, then that is what the relationship is based on. Well, then there is one more bit of decluttering you need to do—that relationship. People who truly love us support us in our highest aspirations. Most people in your life will. Trust that.

Decluttering Expectations and Making Room for Communication: Leah and Rob's Story

Leah and Rob are both seasoned meditators. Their smiles light up a room, and their eyes shine with awareness. As parents of two young children, they take turns going on meditation retreats: one will go while the other stays home to watch the children. They have made a commitment to mindful living, feeling that it is not just important to them as individuals but also as a married couple and as parents.

When I arrive at Leah and Rob's house, we sit down at the table to discuss our decluttering strategy. Their seven-year-old daughter, Amelia, takes out a pad of paper and a pen. As we talk, she occasionally holds up one hand and says, "Hang on. I'm getting this down." Her four-year-old brother, Marco, is less than thrilled about my presence. He is quite certain that I am here to take his toys. I assure him I am not: "We're going to go up to Mommy and Daddy's room today. We're going to teach them how to declutter first. And you'll help us, okay?"

He nods, eyeing me with suspicion. He's not sure I can be trusted. I'm hoping I can show him that decluttering is not about giving away what you love but making room for it.

Leah and Rob's room is in a finished attic in their green-built home. It has all the basic features of a relaxing haven—shining wood floors, high sloped ceilings, and plenty of space to stretch out. But it's not relaxing for either Leah or Rob. The floor is littered with kids' toys, adults' clothing, and quite a few abandoned, unfinished projects.

When I ask the two adults what their intentions are for this room, they tell me: *relaxing, refuge, communication*, and *love*. Amelia writes these words on her notepad. "Our job is to go through this room and remove anything that doesn't resonate with the energy you intend," I tell them.

Amelia looks up from her notes and points her pen at me. "Wait. You're saying that if we find things in this room that don't symbolize those words, they have to go. Is that right?"

"Yes, wise one." I wink at her. "That's right."

I'm interested in the clutter that's sitting out in the room, but I really focus on the twin his-and-hers meditation spaces built into the room. Leah and Rob each have their own private meditation space in their room. Each space is the size of a small walk-in closet, with a door that can be closed. Rob's meditation space is perfectly clear, save his meditation cushion and a blanket. Leah's is another story. There is so much stuff crammed in there that I can barely open the door to see inside. The disparity is striking.

"Okay," I say to the family. "We need to pull everything out of Mom's meditation space so we can see what's in there."

And so we do. (Well, four of us. Marco is still sitting on the floor, playing with his toys. He still doesn't like this decluttering business, and he's still not sure I'm trustworthy).

In the space, we find blankets, boxes, clothing, toys, DVDs, a set of golf clubs given to Leah by her deceased father, stuffed animals that the kids gave Leah to sew, clothing Leah's friends gave her to alter, a guitar that a friend gave to Leah to hold until the friend had settled into her new place. And plenty more.

The common denominator of the clutter blocking Leah's personal breathing room? Expectations. She is burdened by other people's expectations of her, and those people include her husband, her father, her children, and her friends—as well as her expectations of herself. Leah seems to think that it is her job to take on other people's expectations, without question or complaint. None of these assumptions are compassionate toward self or others. All of them just make more clutter.

Dr. Green Weighs In on Leah and Rob's Clutter

In marriages and families, we often make assumptions about what we believe people's roles are. But we do not communicate about our assumptions. Frequently, we form them based on what we've seen our parents do. We take on roles that other people ascribe to us, without question. This can lead to pain and a sense of being burdened.

As meditators, Leah and Rob have learned to look fearlessly at their inner lives in the meditation room, but they have to take their fearlessness and make it work off the cushion, where it counts. This is the real embodiment of the spiritual principles of meditation. Leah and Rob must look at the imbalance that has been created.

It's important to note that this inequity was cocreated. Leah and Rob are equally responsible for the burdens she has assumed for the family. Leah is making sure that Rob's space is clear by taking on clutter for him. Rob feels that he is taking care of his own space and assumes that Leah is taking care of hers. What he doesn't realize is that she is taking on clutter so that he won't have to. Together, they created her clutter, and the kids are following their parents' lead.

Leah has assumed the typical maternal role of family martyr. This is not fair or healthy for anyone in the family. Self-denial leads to dysfunction for everyone. If she suffers in silence, it gives Rob the false impression that maintaining a household is easier than it looks and requires less work than it does. As things are now, she is keeping him in the dark about the amount of work she does. Leah does not want to burden him with it, so she has shouldered the load herself. This is not a good model for their children, who are watching and learning what their parents do. Leah and Rob need to be mutually accountable for fixing the situation.

We all need to take care of ourselves so that others can learn to take care of us. This is a healthy and vital lesson for the whole family, if they are to grow forward together. When one person shifts, those who love her shift around her.

Lauren's Decluttering Session with Leah, Rob, and the Kids

As we sift through the clutter in Leah's meditation space, we realize that each of the items represents a role she assumed unconsciously: her father's hope that she would be a golfer (she is not), her friends' assumption that she is the go-to fix-it person, her children's assumption that she is the only housekeeper in the home, her husband's assumption that she does not want or need help. But now she does need help, and it's wonderful for Leah to see her family pitch in. In the past, she sent them out of the house while she cleaned alone: Rob took the kids out to play, have lunch, or get ice cream while Leah stayed behind to look after everyone's mess. Rob had always assumed this was okay, since Leah never told him it wasn't—she never realized that it wasn't. Through this pattern, the family was split: Leah's work time became everyone else's fun time. It was out of balance.

In the end, Leah's meditation space is restored. They agree to sell the golf clubs at a yard sale. Leah can see that other mementos from her father reflect more appropriate, shared memories of things they mutually loved. The kids' toys are back in their room. The guitar and the sewing projects are going back to her friends. Leah tells Amelia that if she wants her stuffed animal mended, she is happy to show Amelia how to do it by herself. It is great to see this work evolve into a family activity. We all work together. Then we all get to play together. It's really a win-win. Leah is ready to let go of her worry, her fear, her guilt, and her regret—all those *woulds, coulds, shoulds, used-tos,* and *mights*—the burdens that she was taking on for others.

When I leave, I ask Amelia what she learned. She looks down at her notes. "I learned that if you hear yourself saying *I used to, I might, I could,* or *I should* about the things you own, then you are probably going to have to part ways with those things." Awesome.

When they walk me to the door, everyone thanks me but Marco— still worried about giving away his toys. But the following day, Leah calls me to tell me that when she put Marco to bed, he leaned his head on her shoulder and said, "Tell me a story about decluttering, Mommy."

You see? *Shift happens.*

✳   🏠   ♥

Declutter Your Heart by Saying No to Your Mind's Clutter Dumps

Just as there are people who dump trash on your porch, you have voices within you that dump negativity on your heart and expect you to absorb it into your consciousness. These voices of self-judgment and degradation are almost worse than physical clutter. The bags of clothing, spare dishes, and old books that your friends and family leave with you are quiet and benign; for the most part, the people unloading on you are well meaning. But the stuff you dump at the doorway to your heart every day? It is just downright toxic. It is soul corroding.

But just like the "gifts" from your friends, neighbors, and family members, this emotional clutter is just a bunch of unnecessary garbage trying to find a home somewhere. Some negativity is messages from your childhood. Some are messages from outmoded or unquestioned religious, philosophical, or moral beliefs. Some are messages from society. These words hover around the doorway to your heart, waiting for you to have a weak moment, a moment when you are questioning your worth, your energy is waning, or you are distracted by life's cares. Then, these messages come knocking.

Imagine a physical clutter enabler comes knocking at your door with one of those wonderful "gifts" in a big trash bag. If you are tired or distracted, worn out from a hard day's work, you are more likely to wave them in. If you have more energy and awareness, or if you are already in the process of decluttering, you are much more likely to wave them away.

The thought dump is the same way. You've had a long day, and you're already feeling cluttered, tired, and distracted. Your mind shows up at your door with a big bag of self-doubt and self-abuse. "What kind of idiot loses a credit card?" it sneers. "What kind of slob lives in a mess like this? You should be ashamed! You didn't return your friend's phone call? What an ingrate! If you wind up with no friends at all, it will be exactly what you deserve!" If you are too tired to fight off these thoughts, you just wave them on through to your already overburdened heart. You say, "Just dump it right there. I'll sort through it later."

Just as with the actual physical clutter enabler, you need to be aware of what you need and what you don't. You can stop this negativity before it takes root in your heart, saying, "I'm sorry. I'm only accepting positive thoughts." You need to be prepared when your mind brings your heart a big clutter dump. So, right now, while you have the clarity and the energy, we want you to affirm the following statement by writing it down in your journal:

"My heart is a sacred home for the Divine. It is beautiful and whole and meant to be filled with light and nourishment. My dear and noble heart was created to be a refuge in times of trouble. Therefore, I am not accepting any of the following thoughts, which I know to be false. They are toxic clutter and I reject them."

Beneath this statement, we want you to write down the recurring thoughts that show up on the doorstep of your heart when you are tired and distracted. These might be false statements such as "I am incompetent," "I am not worthy of love and kindness," or "I am such an idiot." When you are rested and happy, you know these things are not true. Write them down now, knowing that they are untrue—you're preparing for the moment when you are stressed, overburdened, tired, and distracted. These thoughts will show up to malign you, but you'll have your speech ready. Tell them you're not buying it. Then tell them to hit the road.

Declutter Your Relationships by Saying No to Emotional Clutter Dumps

People in our lives dump on us—even people we love. They dump their daily cares, gossip, petty annoyances, and judgments.

Homes that are decluttered don't really have problems with clutter enablers. Everyone can walk into the home of someone who is uncluttered and see that there is nowhere for the clutter to land. If a clutter enabler showed up with a big box of junk, they would take one look and say, "Never mind. I'm obviously at the wrong home."

You won't be surprised to hear that if you are emotionally cluttered, you will draw other people's emotional clutter. People who have emotional clutter to dump will seek out other emotionally cluttered people to dump on. If you are not certain that this is true, let's do a little thought experiment.

Imagine you have a petty complaint. You were just at the grocery store and the cashier was snapping their gum and refusing to make eye contact, and that kind of behavior just bothers the hell out of you. You just have to tell someone. You feel like you are going to burst if you don't tell someone how much that just annoys you. You walk into an empty room and there are two people standing there: your misanthropic coworker, who right now isn't looking at you because he is on his smartphone posting a snarky comment on Facebook about how annoyed he is about the skimpy froth on his cappuccino. The other person is the Dalai Lama. Which of these two people will you complain to about the rude, gum-snapping cashier who just ruined your day? Most likely, you'll complain to the person who is already ticked off. He would be more than happy to receive this emotional clutter from you. In fact, your negativity fits in very well with his personal inner decor!

As you begin to take care of your own inner clutter, you'll notice that you will draw less and less emotional clutter and clutter enablers. It's as if you were a coatrack: if you have hooks to hang things on, people will hang their stuff on you. If you don't have hooks, they are going to shrug, walk away, and go hang their scarves somewhere else.

In the meantime, get in the habit of not listening to other people's emotional garbage. If they want to talk about what's really wrong, then fine. You are available, but if they are just dumping clutter, resist. You don't even have to tell them, "Sorry, I can't listen to this anymore," though you could say that. All you have to do is just look at them and say, "Hmm." Nothing else. If they don't get a response that is equally dramatic as their complaint, they won't get the satisfaction they are seeking. Just like the coatrack with no hooks, these emotional clutter dumpers will move on.

Declutter Your Roles and Responsibilities by Saying No to Time-Consuming Clutter Dumps

Perhaps you have heard the expression, "If you want to get a job done, give it to the busiest person in the room." If you are a competent and caring individual, it is likely that you have witnessed this axiom manifesting in your own life. Whether you work at an office, out of your home, or at a volunteer organization, you've probably heard the words, "I'm wondering if you can help me with just one more thing." Then, you know what's coming—the person is about to give their work to you, because you have demonstrated a willingness to take on whatever task needs to get done.

If you love the work and it feeds your soul and connects you to love and purpose, then great. Bring it on! But if you say yes while seething with resentment, we encourage you to change your habits. Basically, your coworker arrived at your door with a big bag of responsibilities that he no longer wants to be accountable for—and you have just invited them into your calendar, with a smile on your face. You said, "Put it right over there. I'll take care of it." Can you blame him? Just like a physical clutter enabler, your coworker feels like he's just entered into the best win-win contract ever. He's just unloaded something he doesn't want and you've happily accepted it.

Know what? *You don't have to say yes.* You can say with genuine honesty and grace, "I appreciate your thinking of me, but I have all the work I need at the moment." And it's true. If your life is in balance, you don't need to take anything on that is going to tip the scales. Just as you have the right to keep your home and heart decluttered, you have the right to keep your calendar decluttered. You have no idea how powerful a simple "no, thank you" can be.

21

Principle 6:
Pass Your Clutter Through the
Three Gates of Meaning

Spiritual teacher Eknath Easwaran was influenced in his youth by the words and work of Mahatma Gandhi. As a man committed to peace, he realized that words could be used to either destroy peace or uphold it. Words could be used to inflict wounds or heal them. Because of this, he would instruct his own students that before speaking they should pass their thoughts through three gates:

> The Sufis advise us to speak only after our words have managed to issue through three gates. At the first gate we ask ourselves, "Are these words true?" If so let them pass; if not, back they go. At the second gate, we ask, "Are they kind?" If we still feel we must speak out, we need to choose words that are supportive and loving . . . At the final gate we ask, "Are

they necessary?" They may be true, even kind, but it doesn't follow that they have to be uttered; they must serve some meaningful purpose."[1]

We can use a version of the three gates of speech to help us declutter our words so that when we open our mouths to speak, we offer words of kindness, warmth, and support. We can also use them when we declutter our homes. These gates are:

Is it true to my intentions?
Do I use it?
Is it kind to my heart and spirit?

As we examine any object in our home to decide whether it stays or goes, we can usher it through these three gates.

The First Gate: Is it true to my intentions?

As we mentioned, it's important to be absolutely certain about our intentions. We have to remain clear about precisely the kind of energy we want to create in each room of our home. If an object is not true to the intention of the room, it does not make it through that gate. It needs to find its home in another room where it genuinely reflects the intention of that room, or if it is not true to the intention of any of your rooms, it needs to leave your house altogether.

The Second Gate: Do I use it?

The question is "*Do* I use it?" not "Have I used it?" or "Will I use it?" or "Should I use it?" Almost everything in your house has *some* potential use. Potential use is not one of the gates. *Actual use* is the gate, which means you have used it in the last year.

Remember that we are trying to unburden ourselves of emotional clutter as well. "Have I used it?" indicates wistfulness for the past. "Should I use it?" shows guilt you may feel for buying something that you are not using. "Will I use it?" indicates worry that you may need this object in the future.

"Do I use it?" means "Have I actively been using this for the last year?" If not, it does not make it through the gate.

The Third Gate: Is it kind to my heart and spirit?

Let's go back for a moment to those consuming emotions we talked about earlier. If any object brings up a consuming emotion for you, it is not kind to your heart or your spirit. Your spirit needs sustaining emotions to grow and evolve. If you have objects in your home that make you feel guilt, bitterness, regret, resentment, jealousy, rage, despair, anguish, self-pity, or worry, or if it is a reminder of some trauma in your life, then it does not make it through the third gate.

These gates are not easy to live by. If we use them honestly (whether we are decluttering our hearts, our speech, or our homes), we find that we need to let go of most of what we own, harbor in our hearts, and say to ourselves and others. But if we follow through, we are left with the true treasures of life.

We get in the habit of holding on to things that do not serve us in living happy and fulfilling lives. We would like to think the world is withholding happiness, keeping fulfillment just beyond our reach. But we suggest that maybe happiness and fulfillment have always been in our possession. They have been buried under a wave of clutter that swamped the three gates.

Passing Your Physical Clutter Through the Three Gates

You will need three containers for this exercise: one for each of the three gates. Label the first one, "Is it true to my intentions?" The second, "Do I use it?" The third, "Is it kind to my heart and spirit?"

The first thing you are going to do is line up your three containers from left to right, with the three questions in order. To the left of them, place the possessions you want to take through the three gates. You are going to place one item at a time in each of the baskets, asking the questions of the three gates. If you answer no, then the item stays in the basket. If the answer is yes, it moves on to the next container and the next question. If you can successfully answer yes to all three questions, congratulations! The item has made it through all three gates. You get to hang on to it, because it's not clutter.

This procedure is especially helpful for items that are hard to make a quick decision about. It's a contemplative exercise, so expect to take your time. It will definitely be worth it.

Passing Your Heart Clutter Through the Three Gates

As we have mentioned already, our mental clutter gets into our hearts and takes up residence there without ever proving its worthiness. Think of your heart as the seat of Divine light within you; any clutter you accumulate there ends up blocking that light. Our thoughts make it into our hearts without going through any kind of screening process. We think things like, "My life sucks." Simple. How many of us think this kind of thing without realizing the damage we are doing to our hearts in the process? Your heart sinks and the light within is dampened. That is because you have just dumped clutter in the middle of your temple.

Every temple needs good sentries, and you are going to provide those sentries in the form of the three gates. "My life sucks" wouldn't even get by the first gate. You just got a parking ticket, lost your cell phone, or locked your keys in your car? Okay, that moment sucks. We'll grant you that much. Does that mean your whole life sucks? No. So you've got to turn that thought away at the door. No admittance into the temple.

What kinds of thoughts manage to get all the way in? Let's say someone you love is very sick and you go to the hospital to sit with this person. Again, if you had the thought, "Life is so unfair," it might get through the first gate. It is true. But is it necessary or kind? No. So let's not let that thought enter your heart. How about if you said, "I feel truly blessed to be able to be here with you. What can I do for you?" Does this thought and expression of care make it though all three gates? Yes! It is absolutely true. It is a blessing to be able to be present when a loved one is in pain. It's kind to offer help and necessary to voice it. That thought is worthy of your beautiful, light-filled heart temple.

Not every thought deserves to be in your heart space, and not every thought produces good energy. Take a breath before you voice what's on your mind and pass your thoughts through the gates before you admit them to the beautiful home of your heart. Declutter the thoughts that don't belong.

Passing Your Relationship Clutter Through the Three Gates

Your heart contains profound transformational energy for the world. In truth, all of humanity has a place in your heart. Everyone, regardless of the path he or she walks, is your spiritual brother or sister. Yet, not everyone has your best interest at heart—it's important to know and affirm that.

Some people take the pain of their lives and weave it into wisdom, love, and compassion. They take the proverbial straw of life and spin it into gold. Other people take their pain and turn it into pain for others. We all do this to some degree or another. This is especially true about people before they have any kind of spiritual awakening or awareness. It's even true for people who are spiritually aware—sometimes when we are tired or simply overwhelmed by life, we are not able to take care of our own pain, and inflict it on others.

Of course, there are people who simply have not developed sufficient awareness to transform their pain and suffering into wisdom. We are not saying that everyone in your life has to be a spiritual master or that you should eliminate people from your life who can't transform their suffering into compassion. However, we do caution you not to take their actions personally. (Really, you should not take anyone's actions personally.) But you can use the three gates technique to decide which actions to take into your heart.

Here are your standards for those actions:

- *Is it based on truth?* Does this person see you fully? Do you see him or her fully?
- *Is it kind?* If you take the other person's actions to heart, will this bring more peace to your life or this person's?
- *Is it necessary?* Will engaging with this person's actions bring your relationship to a new level of understanding?

When we find ourselves in the midst of a misunderstanding with loved ones, colleagues, or acquaintances, our interactions should move us in the direction of compassion, peace, and mutual understanding. If an argument moves us away from these gates, then we are moving further and further from the heart. In such cases, we are no longer centered in the heart, but in a shadowy morass of mind clutter, bumping into illusions and cutting ourselves on the jagged edges of unfounded accusations.

The goal in almost any interaction is to welcome people into the temple of the heart, to find true understanding and peace. If this is to be the case, we must be able to show ourselves as whole and see the other person as whole too. We must want peace for ourselves and for them. We must want not just to be understood, but also to understand.

We can attempt to bring others through these gates of truth, kindness, and understanding. However, if their only intention is to lure you into their dangerously cluttered world, even after you have made an honest effort to show them the way of the heart, then you must leave them alone. Wish them well. Pray that they come to no harm. Have compassion for their path, and let them know that the door to understanding is available whenever they choose to use it. Offer them a clutter-free place to meet when they are ready. But in the meantime, don't take their clutter into your heart.

Passing Your Activities through the Three Gates

The three gates for how you spend your time are:

- Is it true to my soul's intention in this world?
- Is it in service to kindness in this world?
- Is it necessary for me to grow?

Almost anything done with proper intention can become a spiritual, soul-shifting opportunity. Every mundane activity in the world can yield spiritual fruit. From chopping vegetables to folding laundry, and from making photocopies at work to helping someone find the canned corn at the grocery store, there is nothing that cannot become a spiritual lesson.

That being said, we have a limited amount of time in this world—although we are under the impression that we have lots of it. Novelist and essayist Anne Lamott tells the story of a time she was out shopping with a terminally ill friend:

> She was in a wheelchair, wearing a wig to cover her baldness, weighing almost no pounds, but very serene, very alive. We were at Macy's. I was modeling a short dress for her that I thought my boyfriend would like. But then I asked whether it made me look big in the hips, and Pammy said, as clear and kind as a woman can be, "Annie? You really don't have that kind of time." And—slide trombone, bells, rim shot—I got it deep in my being.[2]

She's right. We don't have that kind of time. We live under the illusion that we have plenty of time to waste. We think we have time to argue with loved ones, create petty power struggles, share idle gossip, and tear other people down. We think we have time to sabotage our own best efforts. We assume we have hours, days, weeks, months, and years to concern ourselves with whether our hips look big or who left the milk out on the counter or whose hair looked atrocious on Friday night. We use this assumption to delay taking the worthy risks that could change our lives.

We simply don't have time to waste on clutter. Your life is a treasure. The odds that you exist in the first place are miniscule—you truly are blessed with this experience. The Universe in its wisdom has seen fit to give life and consciousness to you. The time you have to live through that gift is finite. So put your time and your heart into what serves you in serving the world. Period. End of story.

Notes:

1. Eknath Easwaran, *Passage Meditation: Bringing the Deep Wisdom of the Heart into Daily Life* (Tomales, CA: Nilgiri Press, 2008), 157.

2. Anne Lamott, *Traveling Mercies: Some Thoughts on Faith* (New York: Anchor Books, 2000), 235.

22

Principle 7:
The Three Standards of True Value—
Happiness, Freedom, Ease

When we help people declutter their homes, the word that comes out of their mouths most frequently is *but*—as in: "But I paid good money for this" or "But I just bought this" or "But this was a gift from my best friend" or "But I inherited this from my grandmother." We are confused about the true nature of value. Money is a symbolic representation of value, but it does not define the value itself. Things are not valuable just because someone paid money for them or because they are old. They are not even valuable if they were passed down through multiple generations.

Objects are valuable in your life if they create happiness, freedom, and ease. If something cost you money, but fills you with regret whenever you look at it, then it does not have value. If a gift needles you with guilt, then it doesn't have value. If someone hands down an heirloom to you that carries the burden of expectation, then it doesn't have value.

If you are constantly feeling drained by regret, guilt, and unfulfilled expectation, then your loss of emotional and spiritual energy is more precious than money. Your energy is the real gold here, and it has true value out in the world. Allowing your energy to be drained—energy that could be used to improve your life and the lives of others—is like throwing gold down the drain.

If any object you possess makes you experience consuming emotions, it is draining your vital energy. If you look at an object in your home and you can literally feel the energy drain out of you, it is using up prime real estate in your home and heart. That space could be better used for love, happiness, joy, and compassion. Think of your heart as if it were a room where you can invite people you love, feed them, and nourish them—a place where you go for comfort, refuge, and refreshment.

Nothing—no matter how much you paid for it, or who gave it to you, or how long it has been in your family—is truly valuable if it is eating up space in your heart that can be used for love, happiness, and freedom. That breathing room is more meaningful than any gift, and it creates a better future than anything you have inherited.

Finding What's Truly Valuable in Your Home

This exercise is actually the reverse of most of our decluttering exercises. For this particular exercise, you are going to take inventory of a particular category of objects and then identify the most valuable one. Since we are spiritually decluttering, we are not looking for the object that has the greatest monetary value or the object that is oldest or has the most history, though it could be those things. We are looking for objects that uphold the three standards of real spiritual value: does it create happiness, freedom, and ease?

For each category of objects (shirts, jewelry, lamps, children's art, books, and so forth), find the one thing that provides you with the most real value. This is the object that makes you smile with your face or in your heart, makes you feel relaxed in your own life, and makes you breathe easy.

The point of this exercise is not to reduce your possessions to one of each category. We are not trying to create a minimalist lifestyle. The point of identifying the single object is to get in touch with why that object feels valuable to you.

So let's say we're going to start with books. You sort through your books and find the one that is the most valuable to you. When you hold it, you feel happy and grateful that it is in your possession. This book makes you smile, relax, and breathe easy. If someone asked you why you chose that particular book, you might say something like, "I find the wisdom in the book refreshing. It takes me to a deep, contemplative place within myself. It reorients me to what's most important." From this information, we might surmise that books are valuable to you when they are refreshing, deep, contemplative, and orient you to meaning. By the same token, if you were looking at your jewelry, you might find value in things that you can dress up or dress down; or perhaps your "most valuable" jewelry reminds you of people you love or an important story in your life.

Using this information about the most valuable object in its category, you are going to measure other objects against it. How do your other objects represent value for you? Let's go back to the example of your favorite book. If the books you value are refreshing, deep, contemplative, and meaningful, we're going to guess that you are holding on to lots of books that do not meet those standards. Maybe you are hoping that they will give you those things that you need—but some books just don't do that for you, and in all likelihood never will. It is like keeping an apple around because you are hoping to squeeze some orange juice out of it. So you can lighten your load by letting go of those books that do not meet your standard of true value.

The same can be said for your other possessions as well. As you read this, you might be thinking: "I paid good money for those books I don't read. I shelled out cold, hard cash for that clothing I don't wear." True. Perhaps you bought the book on spelunking because you read an article that piqued your interest. You went online and bought a book about the best American spelunking adventures completely on impulse, but after you read the first paragraph you realized that you actually hate caves. So why keep a book about something you hate? It doesn't matter how much you paid for it; if it doesn't have real spiritual value to you, it needs to move on.

And here's the great thing: if something doesn't represent real value to you, that doesn't mean someone else won't find value in it. All is not lost. There are spelunkers out there who yearn to go crawling through caves in the United States. They'd love to read your book. What you let go of can be a blessing for others. The true value of those items can be redefined and manifested through their lives.

Now that you understand how true value works, and you understand what you value in each category of items, you will be less likely to buy items that don't meet your standard of value. So the next time you are browsing at the bookstore and come across a book that does not feel deep, contemplative, or meaningful, you can leave it on the shelf. There is no reason to exchange monetary value for something that does not yield real spiritual value.

A Note from Dr. Green

One of the most salient differences between the hoarders I work with and people who are generally cluttered is that hoarders do not perceive a variance in value between any of their possessions—or even between their possessions and their relationships. When faced with a decision to choose between a tangle of wire hangers and a childhood photo album, a hoarder will panic. It's a near-impossible decision for them to make. One hoarder actually became estranged from her adult daughter because her daughter tried to get rid of the collection of wire hangers! But even for people who are more typically cluttered, these kinds of choices can become almost paralyzing. If we don't see that there is a huge spectrum of emotional value among our possessions, we will be faced with a similar sense of anxiety. It is a reflection of a larger issue: being unclear about what is truly valuable in life. Most people who watch the show *Hoarders* are stunned at the way hoarders will choose possessions over relationships—but we all do this at some level when we are unclear about emotional value. If we have the same level of emotional attachment to all of our possessions, it will result in anxiety and confusion. That confusion affects our relationships. Getting clear on what we truly love in our homes is akin to getting clear on what we truly love in our lives.

Finding What's Truly Valuable in Your Heart

Your heart is full of treasures. It's also full of junk. Throughout the day, your heart will reveal its gifts; you'll also trip over some garbage. You need to start getting good at identifying the clutter you're carrying around and what kinds of people, situations, words, media, and food you consume that bring that clutter in.

Take some time to answer these questions in your journal:

- Which emotions bring me happiness, ease, and freedom?
- What people and situations evoke these emotions for me?
- Which emotions deprive me of happiness, ease, and freedom?
- What people and situations typically bring on these emotions?
- What can I do to increase the frequency of emotions that add value to my life, and diminish the emotions that deplete it?

Your answer to the final question is, in essence, your action plan. If we want to experience value in our lives, we have to be proactive about creating it. We cannot passively wait for emotions to overtake us. If we do, we'll find ourselves in constant fear that happiness will leave us or that sadness will overwhelm us. Each of us must see ourselves as the engines for these spiritual and emotional energies. This is emotional empowerment, the key to decluttering and creating emotional value in your heart.

Finding What's Truly Valuable in Your Relationships

Let's talk for a moment about the difference between habits and rituals. Habits are by their very nature unconscious. They are things we do without thinking. We can have good habits or bad habits. Washing your hands before you eat is a good habit. Smoking is a bad habit. We don't really think about either, though one is beneficial to your health and the other destructive.

Ritual, like habit, is a consistent practice, but it relies on a conscious awareness and the intention of validating sacred relationships. Saying "I love you" before you hang up the phone can be a habit or a ritual. It can be a sacred acknowledgment of the relationship or a half-hearted way of saying, "Okay, I have to stop talking now. There's a show I want to watch on TV." It all depends on your intention.

Rituals enrich relationships. Habits kill relationships—even good habits. If a man brings his partner roses every day for ten years, but fails to notice that three years ago she developed a fondness for daisies, his gift will end up making her feel unseen and unloved. When it comes right down to it, habits are nothing but clutter, because they block our ability to truly see one another. A valuable relationship is one that is vital. It shifts with change, and each person sees the other person as constantly evolving. Before Lauren was married, her father gave her some of the best advice she ever received. "You're never married to the person you got married to," he said. "If you expect that person to always be the person you said 'I do' to, you'll find yourself constantly frustrated, resentful, and disappointed."

What we find deeply valuable in a relationship—love, trust, understanding—may always be stable, but how that manifests will change over time. If you have a partner or friend you once loved to go see loud, raucous music shows with, and that is how you express joy together, don't expect that you'll always be in the mosh pit together. The concert is simply an expression of your mutual joy. After a while, if your friend or partner no longer enjoys loud music, that does not mean they have let you down. They have changed—that is all. You probably have as well. That is to be expected. If you truly value that relationship, and if you want to continue to express your joy, love, and understanding, you must be willing to allow the expression of your value to shift in its expression.

Here's the other bit of advice that Lauren's father shared with her: "You know that person who is buying you roses and chocolates and gazing meaningfully into your eyes? That is the same person who is going to be throwing up a bad Chinese meal at three o'clock in the morning. You are going to be the person holding his head out of the toilet. That is true love."

Love is not perfect. Our unreasonable expectation that love has to be perfect in order to be truly valuable? That is clutter too.

Finding What's Truly Valuable in Your Roles and Responsibilities

When Lauren was studying Kabbalah (Jewish mysticism), her teacher, Rabbi Nehemia Polen, told her something that changed her life forever. He told her that each of us is a unique manifestation of the Divine into this world, a light revealed just once in all of Creation. Each person's single most important job is to figure out how to let that light shine. Your roles, responsibilities, and activities are only significant to the degree that they are channels for that light. This idea changed the way Lauren saw the value of her own life and the lives of others around her.

Lauren learned that the best and clearest way you can make your light shine is by doing what you love. If you are a musician, then music is that channel. If you are an artist, it's art; if you are a poet, poetry. But expression is not just about art. If you are a loving parent, then spending time with your children is that channel. If you are good at making money and you use that money to create more value (happiness, freedom, and ease) in the world—then business is the Divine channel. If you adore the plant world, then gardening is your channel.

The bizarre irony of life is that most people will do anything but spend time on activities that broaden that channel of light. We avoid it like crazy. We will do anything we can to avoid it. We would rather clean the house with a toothbrush than do the thing that most effectively channels our inner light. The truth is, we prefer our little stories—the ones comprising petty complaints and incessant grumbling—over the true story of who we are: a unique expression of the Divine light that is our Source. Yet, in order to embrace who we truly are, we must let go of our old beliefs about ourselves.

This is hard because we are more likely to identify with our clutter than the light it covers. Why? We are fearful of letting go of what's familiar. Our egos would have us believe that the story we know is our lifeline; letting go of that story is a kind of death. Marianne Williamson famously quotes a line from *A Course in Miracles* that says, "Our deepest fear is not that we are inadequate. Our deepest fear is that we are powerful beyond measure. It is our light, not our darkness that most frightens us." She goes on to explain her understanding of this statement: "We ask ourselves, Who am I to be brilliant, gorgeous, talented, fabulous? Actually, who are you *not* to be? You are a child of God. Your playing small does not serve the world."[1]

We see this phenomenon of people hiding their light again and again. We have met artists whose studios are tucked away in the farthest reaches of their basements, musicians whose music is lost under piles of unopened mail. We have met parents who promise their children they will go outside and play with them as soon as they are done with some inessential, thankless task. This is no way to live!

Do not tell yourself, "I will open up my inner channel just as soon as I get this other stuff I don't care about out of the way." You have no other time but this time that you are in. You have no time to waste on the inessential. The world is waiting for you. If every person on the face of this earth decided to declutter and shine their inner light fully, what a world we would live in. But that world will not manifest without intention. It will not happen by accident. Each of us needs to take responsibility and give others encouragement to do the same. In the words of Marianne Williamson: "As we let our own light shine, we unconsciously give other people permission to do the same. As we are liberated from our own fear, our presence automatically liberates others."[2]

This exercise is the simplest and the hardest in this book. Are you ready for it? Here goes.

Complete this sentence:

I was born to shine my inner light by _____.

Now go do it. Nothing could be more important to you, to us, and to the world that is waiting.

Notes:

1. Marianne Williamson, *Return to Love: Reflections on the Principles of "A Course in Miracles,"* reissue edition (New York: HarperOne, 1996), 190.

2. Ibid, 191.

23

Principle 8:
Consider Your Legacy
as You Live

What do you want people to remember about you when you are gone? When all is said and done, what do you want your life to be about? No matter what stage of life you are in, this is a good question to contemplate. Decluttering is a way to make the answer clear. What we take away is just as important as what we leave behind.

The act of making daily conscious choices, no matter how small they might seem, is an act of self-determination. With each conscious choice, we are declaring: *This is what is important to me, and this is not.*

Maybe you've had the experience of losing loved ones who did not declutter or sort their belongings before they left this earthly plane. Maybe you sorted through their things and wondered what was really important to them. It was hard to know how to best preserve their legacy. You were afraid to throw anything out, for fear that it might have been important to them. You didn't want to violate their memory by throwing away a key piece of their story.

By making it obvious what is truly important to you, you are making your legacy clear. You don't want the story of who you are buried beneath the rubble of who you are not. Don't leave anyone wondering how to figure that out. By decluttering our lives with the awareness that some day we will pass from this world, and not pretending that we have forever to do it, we are making room to pass on what we know about life while we have time to teach it!

Think of the sages of the world's religions: the most important things they left behind were not their possessions, but their teachings, their compassionate and courageous actions, and the power of their love for humanity. They stripped away everything but what was most important. What is most important has nothing to do with the physical trappings of life. It was their actions and their love. These teachers had great compassion for the generations that followed. They did not want us to flounder or guess at what was important.

And that is the point: decluttering is an act of love and compassion, for the present and the future. It is a selfless act. Each of us must find the courage to do it—for our own benefit, and for the benefit of those who will come after us.

Our stuff tells a story about who we were, who we are, and who we want to be in this world. Everything you own tells some part of your story, but not all parts of the story are significant. Our possessions have varying levels of significance, and so do the stories of how they came into our lives.

When you read a biography of a famous person, the author does not tell you every detail of every story that has ever happened to that person. The biography would be so long, the pages would fill up a whole room. You would have no sense of what that person's life was really about. You would be left to sift through all the stories yourself, hoping that you could make sense of this person's life. The biographer's role is to make sense of that life for you and choose the significant stories, so the reader can understand the fullness of that life. In *Full Bloom: The Art and Life of Georgia O'Keeffe*, biographer Hunter Drohojowska-Philp tells the story of young Georgia wandering the roads of her native Sun Prairie, Wisconsin, where her father owned farmland:

> She could stroll the dirt lanes for hours and not see a building or a field that didn't belong to her family. In the spring and the summer, wildflowers bloomed against the wire and wood-post fence beyond which plains rolled out to an unbroken horizon. In the fall and winter months, she looked out her bedroom window at the broad, gun-metal sky. This land left an impression of spatial grandeur on young Georgia and she would ever credit it as being integral to, even crucial in, her development as an artist.[1]

Georgia O'Keeffe probably did other things in her young life besides staring out her window at the beauty of nature. She brushed her hair and teeth. She had to learn to add and subtract. She ate vegetables. She scrubbed pots and pans. She fell down and scraped her knees. She argued with her siblings. In many ways, she was like all other children. So why does the biographer choose to tell the story of Georgia O'Keeffe walking through the fields, letting the landscape soak into her soul? Because it is a significant story that helps the reader understand the adult Georgia O'Keeffe, whose art we love. It connects her early age with the vision of a twentieth-century visionary. This has deep significance—the other childhood experiences, probably not. Biographers piece together stories, like breadcrumbs of meaning, that lead to the icon we all know.

Your life is also full of significant stories—but if you are cluttered, your significant stories are probably buried beneath your insignificant ones. Over time, the things we own pass out of usefulness. Some of these items are significant. Others are not. The ridiculously nerdy sci-fi novel you both read multiple times (and practically memorized) that sparked the very first conversation you had when you realize you'd finally met your soul mate? That is an object with a significant story. The first love letter your beloved wrote to you is a possession with a significant story. That would appear in your biography, would it not?

Now, consider a pair of ticket stubs to the matinee of a movie neither of you actually enjoyed and which you both wished you hadn't wasted your time or money on. Those ticket stubs do not say much about who you are, who you love, or what you are committed to. They don't tell a significant story. But if you are a clutterer, it's very possible that they are crammed in the same drawer as your love letter, along with rubber bands, expired coupons, and the broken necklace you have been meaning to repair for the last two years. If others sifted through that drawer, they would have trouble deciphering the meaning of your life.

You are the biographer of your own life. It's your job to tell your story, to find and highlight the essential meaning of your life. Don't leave it for other people to figure out after you're gone. Tell it now! Make it your priority. Remember, decluttering is not just making the meaning of your life clear to others—it is about making the meaning of your life clear to you!

✳ 🏠 ♥

Releasing Guilt and Making Room for Happiness:
Sandra's Story

Sandra and her husband, Jeff, call it "The Shed." But they say the name as if were the title of a horror movie: "The . . . SHEEEEEEEEDDD!"

I am standing in Sandra's kitchen sipping a cup of tea. All around us are emblems of Sandra and Jeff's spiritual lives: crystals, dreamcatchers, and totem carvings. The two of them are shamans, trained in the way of traditional spiritual healing methods of the native people of this continent. They understand deeply how important the quality of energy is. Part of their work is cleansing physical spaces affected by negative energy and trauma. But The Shed is another story. They just pretend it doesn't exist.

"When I need anything out of The Shed, I basically avert my eyes, get what I need as quickly as I can, and get out of there just as fast," Sandra says.

"Well, do you want to show it to me?" I ask.

"Are you sure?" She winces. "Maybe today is not a good day. It's kind of rainy."

"It's as good a day as any." I smile.

Sandra closes her eyes, takes a deep breath, and lets it out slowly. Then, she says, "Okay. Let's go. You ready?"

"As I'll ever be," I assure her.

As she reaches for the handle on the storage shed, she looks back at me for reassurance. I nod to her, and Sandra opens the door slowly. Exactly like a horror movie.

It's not nearly as bad as I expected. It just looks like a typical gardening shed. I tell Sandra that, but I also share with her that it doesn't really matter what her clutter looks like on the outside. It's how it feels to you on the inside. If Sandra's shed sends shivers up her spine or makes her skin crawl—clutter alert.

Along with gardening tools, there are some ghosts from the past hanging around in here. I see skis that Sandra used as a teenager, dress-up clothes that once belonged to her now-adult daughter, Halloween costumes worn by her son, and a box of china from her great-grandmother that Sandra has no use for (and which her daughter has told her in no uncertain terms that she does not want).

"Can I show you just one more thing?" she asks.

"Sure," I tell her, "lead the way."

I follow Sandra around the corner, and she puts her hand on an antique mahogany headboard. When she touches it, her jaw tenses and her eyes narrow. "I hate this. I really do. I hate it."

She tells me that when her grandmother passed away, Sandra flew out to the funeral. She was allowed to pick one thing to keep from her grandmother's home. At the time, she had her daughter (then about ten years old) with her. Her daughter chose the mahogany bed. Sandra questioned the wisdom of picking something so large. She had something small in mind, like a brooch. But she didn't want to disappoint her daughter, so the bed became Sandra's inheritance. Her father rented a truck to drive the heavy piece to Sandra's home.

From that moment on, the bed was nothing but trouble for her. Being an antique, it was not made to fit a standard-sized mattress. When they tried to put her daughter's mattress in it, it wouldn't quite fit. "It was forever falling apart. For years! Honestly, I felt resentful. Every time I had to put that darned bed back together, I thought, *Why didn't someone tell me that it was not standard-sized? Why didn't they warn me how much trouble it was going to be?*"

When Sandra's daughter moved off to college, the bed went into The Shed.

"So why haven't you just let it go, if you hate it so much and it brings up so many negative feelings?" I ask, though I already know the answer.

"I just can't make myself," she says, shaking her head and looking down woefully at the headboard. "I'd feel too guilty. I'd feel like I was ungrateful for this huge gift and for the people who took all the time and money and trouble to bring it to my house. I'd feel like I was dishonoring my grandmother's memory." Sandra sighs.

"What do you think I should do?" she asks.

Dr. Green Weighs In on Sandra's Clutter

When we look at inheritance, it's essential that we find ourselves in right relationship with our ancestors. We have inherited so much from our ancestors: deep and indispensable wisdom, yes, but also brazen foolishness. Love, yes. But also petty grudges and unexamined prejudices. Courage, yes. But also untested and paralyzing fears. It all sits around in the attic of your unconscious, mixed together. As if it all mattered and is worth hanging on to. We make the assumption that the best way to honor our ancestors is to keep everything they give us. But if something (physical, emotional, or spiritual) that you inherited is causing you pain or discomfort, you are not honoring them, their spirit, or their memory. Don't make the mistake of assuming that because something is generations old, it is inherently valuable. Only keep what you truly want to pass along to the next generation. If it's not creating happiness, then it is not honoring anyone's memory.

We have the misapprehension that honoring our ancestors' sacrifices means holding on to every decision they made, every attitude they had, and every possession they owned. Causing yourself guilt or pain over their possessions dishonors their hope for your present happiness and future freedom. Your ancestors truly wanted (and continue to want) your happiness, freedom, and unapologetic, radical love for yourself. Love yourself the way they would love you—the way they do love you.

Lauren's Decluttering Session with Sandra

As shamans, Sandra and Jeff understand being in right relation to ancestry.

"Do you believe that any of your ancestors would want you to spend so many years in torment over something so simple as a headboard?" I ask Sandra.

"No. But what am I going to do? I can't just give it away to Goodwill. It's worth a lot. But I wouldn't feel right taking money, either. It would feel like I were selling out my family history for cash." Sandra knows she needs to let the headboard go, she just doesn't know how to do it.

"Here's what I suggest," I tell her. "You know that your grandmother would want nothing but happiness for you and for all future generations, right?"

"Yes," she answers. But it almost sounds more like a question. She is not sure where I am leading her. She is committed to honoring the past, and she does not want to be led away from her commitment, nor do I want to lead her astray. I want her to let go in a way that honors the past, her present, and her future.

"Then sell the bed. Someone who loves antiques will be so happy to find it. It's still a beautiful piece of furniture and it doesn't carry any emotional weight for them, as it does for you. They'll be absolutely overjoyed. Then you take the money and open up a college fund for your future grandchildren. That way, you can take what was given to you by the past generation and transform it to happiness and enlightenment for the future generation. You become the bridge between those generations. There is no greater honor you can give to the past than taking care of the future."

"Oh my goodness," Sandra says, exhaling deeply, "what a huge relief." She is smiling now. Her eyes are shining. And her shoulders relax, as if she is no longer carrying the burden of the past on them.

✳   🏠   ♥

Saving Your Legacy by Decluttering Your Home

You are going to rescue your legacy from the grips of the inconsequential. You are going to tell the story of who you are, for your own sake and for the generations that follow you. It doesn't matter where you are in your life. It doesn't matter if you are just out of college and working your first job or if you are recently married and thinking about having your first child, if you are about to send your first child off to college or if you are a grandparent whose kids and grandkids visit on the weekends. No matter where you are, start telling the story of who you are now and get in the habit of removing the insignificant details as soon as you realize they are irrelevant.

For this exercise, you will need a large plastic container that can be tightly sealed. You are going to create a memory box. You are going to put into the container the objects that tell significant stories of how you came to be who you are in this moment.

First, use your journal to answer these three important questions:

- Who am I in this moment?
- Who was I before I arrived in this moment?
- Who do I want to become?

These aren't easy questions, and you might have a lot to say about each of them. You might also find yourself stumped by them. All of that is quite all right. These are questions of deep significance; in the midst of a busy and full life, we don't often stop to ask ourselves these things. But they are so important because your story and your legacy become clear in the process of answering them.

Right now we ask that you really focus on the "Who was I?" question and make some solid, clear decisions about which items speak significantly to your identity and which items do not.

If you find an object that speaks to who you are now or who you want to become in the future, then it can stay out. However, examine the objects that you think represent your past self. Deciding is amazingly simple. When you have something in your hand that belongs in the category of "who I once was," ask yourself, "Does this tell a significant story of who I once was?" If your answer is no, then the item goes to the trash, recycling, or donation pile. If the answer is yes it can stay out on display, or go into your memory box. You can even write the story down on an index card and either pin the card to the item or put the item in a clear plastic bag with the story.

If you're not sure if the story is truly significant, tell it to someone in your life whom you trust. Ask him if it rings true about who he knows you to be. Ask him if it is a story that he would retell to another person about you.

Again, no matter who you are, how old you are, or where you are in your life, it is never too early to begin this important reflective process. You'll come to know yourself better through it. Ultimately, the people who care about you will come to know you better as well.

Saving Your Legacy by Decluttering Your Heart

In this chapter, we are looking at your life as if you were writing your autobiography, so decide: is your story an endless, meaningless struggle, or a story of the triumph over meaninglessness? Is it going to be a story of regret or of fulfillment? Is it going to be a story of clarity or a murky, indecipherable mess?

The late and great Rabbi Abraham Joshua Heschel, dear friend and ally of Dr. Martin Luther King Jr., a person who loved God and humanity as much as a human being possibly could, was asked shortly before his death for the advice he would give to young people just getting their start in life. He said, "Remember that there is meaning beyond absurdity. Know that every deed counts, that every word is power . . . and above all that you must build your life as if it were a work of art."[2]

Your life is a work of art that begins in your heart. You are the sculptor. In order for it to take form and to convey beauty you must carve out the pieces that do not matter. Artwork lasts beyond the life of the artist. Hearts outlive the bodies they were housed in. If you want your heart to live on—in the form of what Eastern religions and philosophies call karma, the energy of action that drives cause and effect—what do you want to live on? Your courage or your fear? Your love or your hatred? This question is beautifully answered by Zen master Thich Nhat Hanh:

When a cloud is polluted, the rain is polluted. So purifying thoughts, word, and action creates a beautiful continuation. We can see the effects of our speech in our children. My disciples are my continuation—both monastic and lay. I want to transmit loving speech, action, and thought. This is called karma in Buddhism.

This body of mine will disintegrate but my karma will continue—karma means action. My karma is already in the world. My continuation is everywhere in the world. When you look at one of my disciples walking with compassion, I know he is my continuation. I don't want to transmit my negative emotions, I want to transform them before I transmit them. The dissolution of this body is not my end. Surely I will continue after the dissolution of this body.[3]

You have a choice of how you'll continue in the future, by mindfully choosing your actions today. It's not that we won't feel fear or hatred or have cluttered feelings or thoughts. You can choose whether to give voice to those thoughts or act on those feelings. If you consciously choose to be loving rather than hateful, the karma of that love is carried forward. Love is not just a feeling: love is a verb. Love is an action. Peace, joy, understanding, courage, and strength are all actions.

What do you want your life to be about, and what are you willing to remove in order to make its meaning clear? Take out your journal and complete these sentences:

I want my life to be about _____.
I am willing to remove _____ in order to
        make it clear that this is what my life is about.

Rabbi Heschel said, "Start working on this great work of art called your existence."[4]

Your whole life is ahead of you. Start building the work of art that is your life now. Start where it counts—in your heart!

Saving Your Legacy by Being Grateful for Your Relationships—Both Positive and Negative

Every person whose life is written up in a biography has known influential people. Some are advocates and allies; others are foils, but all of them are crucial to the story of that person's evolution. Our lives are just the same. Every person we encounter has something to teach us about who we are becoming. Some people teach us who to be by example. Others teach by negative example, by showing us how not to be. In a deep sense, all of these people are our gurus. A guru is a teacher whose being is a mirror to your Self. They hold up a mirror, saying: *Look at who you are. Look at who you are not.* The guru burns away illusions of Self, so what you are not falls away and what you are shines clearly.

Some gurus will teach you lessons about who you are. You want to stay with those gurus. Walk in their path. Your gratitude is expressed by your desire to keep them close, as a reminder of who you are and who you want to be. Other gurus will teach you lessons about who you don't want to be, who you don't want to become. To such gurus, we silently bow in thanks for the lesson, and then we walk away. Every person has a lesson to teach. For some of those people, the greatest lesson they teach us is how to say goodbye.

List the gurus who have taught you about who you are. In your heart, or out loud if they are still present in your life, say thank you for what they've taught you and continue to teach you. Be clear about what they have taught you in life.

Now, list the gurus in your life who have taught you what you are not. In your heart, bow to them and release them from their duty. Be clear about what they have taught you. It's just as important as the lessons your positive gurus have taught you. Do for them what they taught you to do: tell them goodbye.

Saving Your Legacy by Decluttering How You Spend Your Time

What are you doing with your days? Is it biographical material? Let's be fair and honest. Most of what we do is not earth-shattering. But some of it is, and sometimes the stories of who we are and what we are becoming get lost in the mindless babble, gossip, and complaints of our daily drudgery. We're going to ask you a question and we want you to be completely honest in your answer. Imagine you've come home at the end of a long day. Your beloved or your friend asks you how your day was. Are you more likely to crow or complain? Are you going to tell them the most interesting part of your day, or are you going to drone on about some irritation you encountered? If you answered the latter, you are not alone. Most people—even if almost everything went right—are going to tell you about what went wrong.

Before you launch into an account of your daily drama, maybe you should check to see if the things you are complaining about are actually blessings. Here's a reflection from Lauren on the subject:

Am I burdened? Or am I blessed?

I have a house to clean. I have children to shuttle around. I have a job that needs to be attended to. I have money that I am not managing as well as I could. I have tons of friends I just can't seem to keep up with. There are times when I feel I can barely keep my head above water. Trust me: it's not a comfortable feeling. Not at all.

Yesterday, I was going to get on Facebook and gripe about how busy I was.

But then, I stopped and realized that if I remove the second half of each of those complaints, I am left with the following true statements:

I have a house. I have children. I have a job. I have money. I have tons of friends.

What am I complaining about? These are not burdens. These are blessings.

Yes, I am busy. And yes, there are times I feel overwhelmed. But if I am mindful, I realize that the reason I am so busy is that I am blessed with abundance. Can it be overwhelming? Yes, sometimes.

But would I want the opposite? No job? No friends? No family? No money? No home?

It's often the case that when we complain, we are actually complaining about blessings.

When I shared this thought with a friend recently, she offered that she had too much work to do. She remarked that if she cut that statement in half, she was left with either "I have too much" or "I have work." You could definitely do worse.

When my children's hair grows a little too long, I can't see their faces beneath the curtain of hair that has grown over their eyes. It's not that their bright and shining eyes have disappeared; it's just that they are covered. A simple trim and suddenly I can see their eyes, gaze into them, and smile at them once again. Trimming our complaints like this allows us to see the blessing shining from behind the burden. Give your complaints a little trim and see the blessing within.

Your job now is to take a look at your so-called burdens and give them a trim so you can see the blessings that reside underneath.

Notes

1. Hunter Drohojowska-Philp, *Full Bloom: The Art and Life of Georgia O'Keeffe* (New York: W.W. Norton & Company, 2005), 20.

2. Abraham Joshua Heschel, *I Asked for Wonder: A Spiritual Anthology*, ed. Samuel Dresner (New York: Crossroad Publishing, 1983), ix.

3. Thich Nhat Hanh, "What Happens When You Die?" (talk presented at a spiritual retreat, Hong Kong, May 15, 2007), *Breathwork*, http://www.breathwork.be/articles /breathwork/199-birth-and-death-v15-199.

4. Krista Tippet, "The Spiritual Audacity of Joshua Heschel," *On Being with Krista Tippet*, transcript, December 6, 2012, http://www.onbeing.org/program/spiritual -audacity-abraham-joshua-heschel/transcript/4951.

24

....

Principle 9:
No More Hiding Places

We all have places in our homes and our hearts where we hide the stuff we don't want other people to see. Everyone does this. There is a really powerful, self-perpetuating irony in this behavior. We all believe that we are the only ones with clutter to hide. We go to other people's homes and it appears that they have no clutter. Their surfaces are clear and everything seems in its place. So we all think: *I am the only one.* And what does this make us want to do? It makes us want to hide our clutter, that's what!

So everyone is hiding their clutter based on the false belief that no one else has clutter (because everyone is hiding their clutter from everyone else). Look, if everyone had the courage to take all their clutter and dump it in the middle of their living room—every closet, drawer, space under every bed, shelf, and cabinet—we would all see the reality. That shocking reality is that we are all human and everyone's life gets messy and unmanageable from time to time.

This goes for heart clutter as well. We all carry around heart clutter: fears, worries, insecurities, and disappointments. It may appear to you that you are the only person who carries these burdens. It seems like everyone else is perfectly happy, has a well-organized emotional life, and is spiritually clear. Operating under this false assumption, we take the same approach in our hearts as we do in our home. We stash clutter away and hide it. We tuck it all into secret hiding places that only we know about. Just as with our homes, it may be that even the people we live with don't know where our secret hiding places are or what's crammed away in them. In fact, it may be the case—and we see this with many clutterers—that we have stashed away so much stuff, that we no longer know what's in there. We don't know our full emotional inventory any more than we know what's in our home.

Because of these hiding places, we are in the habit of being spiritually dishonest. Whatever Higher Power we feel connected with, we can't even be honest with that sacred being. We are so committed to presenting a clean and clear front, so used to guarding these private hiding places within ourselves, that we cannot even open ourselves completely to the very power that can heal us.

We want to suggest that you open up your hiding places and let the lights of day, spirit, and healing shine on them. There has to be an honest inventory in our homes and our hearts. The image we present to the world of who we are and how we live is just that—an image. It is an image until we stop hiding who we are and stop trying to pretend our homes and our hearts aren't cluttered and disordered. If we have the constant anxiety that we are about to be discovered for who we truly are, there is no way that we can truly relax. No amount of polishing up the exterior will do away with the fear that someone is going to stumble into one of our dreaded hiding places and fully know who we are.

If you remember one thing, let it be this: You are loved. By your Creator. By the Universe. By All That Is. And not just for the parts of you that are shining and inviting. You are loved—even the parts of you that feel messy, unfinished, frayed, or unclear. We are loved, all of us, for being human and imperfect as we truly are.

There is no need to hide what needs to be forgiven. You are already forgiven. You now need to forgive yourself. Open up the hiding places. Reveal yourself. You can't declutter until you've taken this courageous step: the act of opening in pure faith.

No More Hiding Places in Your Home

The longer you keep your hiding places secret, the more treacherous they become. Think of the closet that you open just a crack, shove your possession in, and close as quickly as possible. Think of the junk drawer that you don't want to reach into because you don't know if you are going to be cut by a sharp edge or poked with a sewing needle. Think of your garage or your attic, stacked so high with boxes that one small misstep might send them tumbling down on top of you.

When you started using that hiding place, it wasn't so treacherous. You thought, *I'm not sure if I want to keep this thing or get rid of it—and even if I kept it, I don't really have a place for it so I am just going to stick it in the attic for now.* Well, "for now" has turned into years. One thing has turned into hundreds, possibly thousands, of delayed decisions.

So we have to empty out our hiding places and commit to no more hiding. There's no easy way to do this, folks. You have to just open it up, drag out the contents, and see what's inside.

Just so you know—don't get freaked out—we're going to tell you right up front what's in there. You're going to find evidence of your worries, fears, guilt, regret, insecurities, and unprocessed grief. How do we know that you are going to find those things? We know that because *you are hiding them*. We don't usually hide what we love. We hide what we are afraid to face and are afraid to deal with.

If it is just a drawer, dump it out. If it is a closet, pull out everything and lay it on the floor. If it is your attic, basement, or garage, you'll need to commit to one box a day and stick with it. Whatever the box contains, you need to release it. Yes, we know it's frightening. We know it's the last thing you want to do. But this is about you coming clean with yourself. This is about you living openly and honestly with yourself and others. There is no relief greater than that.

This is how you are going to go through your big secret dump, now that it is out of hiding. You must tell yourself the following things:

- I am no longer going to hide my fear from myself or others.
- I am no longer going to hide my insecurities from myself or others.
- I am no longer going to hide my worries from myself or others.
- I am no longer going to hide my guilt from myself or others.
- I am no longer going to hide my grief or sadness from myself or others.

You need to decide once and for all that you are not going to live with these things. In previous exercises, you have learned to identify objects that resonate with negative energy. As we've said, your hiding places are going to have lots of negative energy in them, so you'll need to get these things out of your home, heart, and life. We don't care if they are out of sight. They are not out of mind. They are not out of heart. Even if nobody else knows they are there, these things are consuming you.

Get yourself two big ol' bags: a donation bag and a garbage bag.

As you go through these hidden objects, you need to clearly identify what consuming emotion they represent. It is important to become aware of which consuming emotions are predominantly driving your need to hide. Remember that all of our physical clutter is a manifestation of our emotional clutter. If you find you are primarily hiding things that make you feel guilty, then it is important to recognize that guilt has too much underlying power in your life. If you notice that you tend to hide things that make you feel worried, then perhaps worry is something you are trying to push down or away. So, as you place each object in the bag, you need to say something like: "These dress-up clothes that once belonged to my daughter bring up wistfulness for the past. I no longer want to feel wistful about the past. I want to live in the present, the only moment in which my happiness can manifest." You might say: "These neckties that belong to my ex-husband bring up resentment for being betrayed by him and grief for the love I lost. I no longer want to live with resentment about the past or grief for what is gone. I want to live in the present, the only moment in which my happiness can manifest."

Whatever you are hiding is taking away from your happiness. No more secrets. It's time to let them go so your happiness can manifest in this present moment—the only moment you truly have.

No More Hiding Places in Your Heart

Looking into your heart can be even more terrifying than looking into a cluttered closet or a dank basement. The buildup of emotions that we keep in our hearts can be even more treacherous territory than the physically cluttered places in our homes. Have you ever told a story from your childhood—not a traumatic event, just some petty annoyance—like the way your brother always claimed the best slice of meat for himself at dinner without ever asking if you wanted it, or how your teacher in second grade never called on you, no matter how high you raised your hand?

When you tell this story, do you feel your anger and irritation rising as if it were happening all over again? This might have happened twenty, thirty, forty years ago, but you still feel your neck get hot. You still want to give your brother or your teacher a piece of your mind. But then you realize, deep down, that they are not there for you to complain to (and even if they were, it would be a little late to be bringing it up). So you push it back into the closet of your heart. The unfortunate thing is, if you keep hiding these emotions, they will crop up at the most inopportune time.

Maybe your boyfriend reaches for the biggest slice of cake without asking and you blow up at him. You accuse him of being the most selfish person on earth. He looks at you like you've lost you mind. Or your boss doesn't call on you in a staff meeting, and you seethe at the injustice. You're not mad at your boyfriend or your boss. You're mad at your brother and your teacher.

So when we feel these uncomfortable feelings, whether they are irritation, anger, sadness, or fear, you are going to learn to not push them away. You are going to coax them out of their hiding places and let them know that you are there for them.

Here is the simple prescription. You will say, as you would to a small child who is trying like crazy to get your attention, "Hello, [difficult or uncomfortable emotion]. I see you are there. I know you are in pain. I am here to take care of you."

No more pushing emotions in the closet. No more emotions jumping out at inappropriate times. Just a simple acknowledgment. Bring these emotions out into the light, where they can be seen. Remember, we're not dealing with monsters that need to be battled here. We're dealing with small, frightened children that need to be attended to. Be the adult. Don't push them away.

No More Hiding Places in Your Relationships

"What's wrong?"

"Nothing."

How many times have you had this conversation? Something is obviously wrong, but it is not being acknowledged. Hiding places do not work in healthy relationships. Never have. Never will.

One of the reasons we tend to play the game of hide-and-seek in relationships is that we feel that if someone truly loves us, understands us, and cares about our well-being, they ought to be able to intuitively know what we are feeling. Do you know what that is called? It's an assumption. And you know what assumptions are in relationships, don't you? That's right. They're clutter. Love does not make anyone a mind reader.

We hide ourselves because we want desperately to be found. It's ridiculous, this game. It's like playing hide-and-seek and not telling the other person you're playing. Of course, no one is going to come look for you if they don't know you're hiding. Stop playing games. If you want to be found, come out into the light where you can be seen. Don't expect people to prove their love to you by hunting for your feelings.

Are you hurt? *Say you are hurt.*

Are you lonely? *Say you are lonely.*

Are you afraid? *Say you are afraid.*

Relationships are doomed in the shadows—but they thrive in the open.

No More Hiding behind Excuses

Part of the way we clearly express who we are is by what we choose to do with our time. The other way we clearly say who we are is by what we choose not to do with our time. We often create the clutter of misunderstanding by making excuses for why we choose not to participate in certain activities or take on certain obligations. There is nothing wrong with saying no. Of course we are all fearful of hurting someone else's feelings when we do. We don't want them to take it personally. Most of the time, it's truly not personal, but one thing is guaranteed: it will be taken that way if you make an excuse and get caught in it. Throughout this book, we have encouraged you to learn to say no, and we hope you have been practicing. Now we must learn to say no without making excuses. It is just another measure of your innate courage and your willingness to shine through in your beautiful essence.

When you say no, it's important to be honest and forthright about what your priorities are and why this particular activity or role does not fit into your life at the moment. Part of our spiritual development has to do with being honest and clear with ourselves and others. Your word is your bond and your power. Words have the remarkable ability to manifest into the world. Genesis 1:1–31 tells us that the Divine One spoke this world into existence. Your words also hold the power to form your existence.

No hiding behind excuses.

This is a simple formula that you can use:

Thank you for asking me to _____.
    Right now, I am focusing my time and energy on
_____, so I am
going to have to decline, though I do appreciate the offer.

What are your other options? Saying yes and feeling resentful or regretful? We already know that is emotional clutter. Making up a lie and getting caught or living in fear of being caught? That is clutter as well! Anything but honesty is bound to create clutter in your heart or in your relationships. You can't afford either.

You can only afford honesty—with yourself and others.

Principle 10: Your Home Is Already Uncluttered—
It Is in Its Nature to Be That Way

Underneath it all, your house is already uncluttered. Before you moved into your home, it was perfectly empty. This is the pure and natural state of your home: to be absolutely open and full of potential. When you moved in, you brought what was essential to live a healthy, happy life: furniture to rest on, beds to sleep on, pots and pans to cook with, washcloths and towels, clothing to keep you warm and dry, books to fill your mind with fascinating ideas, and a desk to process the work of your home's upkeep.

Then—perhaps out of a sense of insecurity or a fear that your basic needs would not be provided for, or perhaps from a core lack of understanding or indecisiveness about what you really needed—you began to accumulate clutter. Now you have too much furniture. You might think that if you're not feeling rested it's because you don't have the right things to rest on. You collect kitchen implements, assuming that if you're not feeling fully nourished, it's because you have the wrong gadgets. You have too many toiletries because you're not feeling naturally beautiful and deeply refreshed, so that must mean you haven't found the right cleanser or the perfect shade of makeup.

But beneath all the stuff, your true home waits to be uncovered: open, shining, clean, and full of the potential to make you feel happy and safe. You see, in the drive to become relaxed, we have created more work for ourselves. In the effort to help ourselves to fast-and-easy nourishment, we have crowded out the potential for real, deep satisfaction. In our search for beauty, we are bypassing our true, innate beauty. In our hunt for wisdom and inspiration, we have forgotten that we are the source of wisdom and inspiration. In our fear that we may lose track of what we need to be happy, we have lost track of happiness.

Your heart is precisely the same. When you were born into this world, your heart was absolutely pure, clean, open, and uncluttered. But life takes over very quickly, and even in our first moments, our minds start making demands to ensure our survival. From the moment that we first drew breath, we cried out for warmth, food, love, and attention. Some of us may have had parents who were able to provide for us with ease and grace. Others of us may have found ourselves in a continual struggle to have our basic needs met. All of us have received messages from the time we were small about what represented safety, warmth, nourishment, and love—some of these messages were true, while others were false.

Some beliefs we took on furthered our sense of security and helped us draw closer to our heart's true nature. Some beliefs we were exposed to induced greater insecurity and pulled us away from our hearts' sustenance. Over time, all of our hearts, like our homes, have become cluttered with beliefs, stories, and emotions that are not only unnecessary, but are also perhaps dangerous to our well-being. Underneath it all—the insecurities, demands for unmet needs, unfulfilling beliefs—there is your heart, with its pure and beautiful nature, waiting to be uncovered and revealed in all its shining beauty.

This is the beauty of decluttering. It is like a treasure hunt. We are uncovering the treasure of the true nature of your home and your heart. We are removing what is unnecessary and revealing what has always been there: the potential for sustenance and beauty that is sitting patiently, smiling.

One of the things that gets in the way of our living uncluttered is that we are in the habit of seeing the clutter everywhere we look. We cannot imagine it being any other way. We believe the nature of a drawer is to be full; the nature of a closet is to hold clothes; and the nature of a cabinet is to contain, well, contents. Actually, the true nature of these spaces is to be absolutely empty.

Buddhist masters have taught us that the nature of the mind is to be empty. Thoughts may fill minds—indeed, they may fill them to bursting—but the essential nature of the mind is to be empty. The purpose of meditation is to witness the essential emptiness of mind. Hard to believe, we know.

We want you to clear something out and keep it clear. For no other reason than to show it is possible.

It's essential that there is some place in your house that stands as a testament to your personal commitment to holding space open for yourself. Commit to the notion that not every open space needs to be covered or filled. We may agree to this theoretically, but our behavior tells a different story. We bet that your home, whether it is a three-hundred-square-foot studio apartment or a rambling mansion, is packed to the gills. Every flat surface is covered. Every drawer is stuffed. Every closet is full. And it's no wonder. We've been taught from the time we were small that this is how these spaces are supposed to be utilized; it's counterintuitive to do anything else. We believe this to the extent that we instinctively fill any open space we find with more stuff.

Imagine that tomorrow you wake up and realize that you have another closet that you never knew was there, an open space with no purpose whatsoever. What would be the first thing you would do? You would fill it up! If you discovered a closet without a purpose, the first thing you would do is find a purpose for it. Worse, you might just dump overflow junk into it with no plan whatsoever—which, if you are being honest with yourself, is probably exactly what would happen.

The places in our homes that collect the remnants of our indecision, distraction, and anxiety are what author and decluttering coach extraordinaire Marla Cilley (aka FlyLady) calls "hotspots." They are the places that collect the stuff that we don't have the time or energy to deal with (or are just downright fearful of). They are monuments to our lack of mindfulness.

This empty space that you are about to create is going to be the most mindful space in your house. Because it is the most mindful space, it is also the most compassionate space because you are leaving room for nothing. *For. No. Thing.*

Well. There is one thing we want you to put on this counter or into this drawer or closet or shelf. We want you to place some reminder of life's inherent wisdom, beauty, or love in the space. Perhaps it is a simple, fresh flower. Perhaps it is a photo of a family member who has transitioned from this life—the person who always loved and embraced you, without condition or question—or a beloved spiritual master. Perhaps it is your representation of the

Divine Oneness, whether that is a statue of Jesus or a favorite saint, a painting of Krishna or a bodhisattva, or a photograph of nature that speaks to your understanding of Mother Earth's timeless and loving wisdom. That symbol is there to remind you of what is most important. What is most important stays primary.

And it works too. If you chose a photograph of your grandmother (who always smelled like a blend of rosewater and fresh baked bread—and no matter how sad or angry or rebellious you were, always drew you into her arms, buried her face in your hair, and told you that you were like sunshine that made the flowers bloom and the green grass grow), are you going to dump your unopened mail there? Mindlessly throw a pocketful of change in front of her? Distractedly drop the take-out food menu that was rolled up in your door handle when you arrived home from work? No way. You are not going to return her kindness, care, undying love, and compassion with mindless, distracted dumping! This is, in essence, sacred ground in your home.

Your grandmother loved you beyond the stars. Jesus loves you completely. Bodhisattvas walk the path of compassion and courage to show you that fearless living is the path to freedom. Your spiritual master pours out wisdom for the constant improvement of your being. Nature cares for you ceaselessly. How will you repay these compassionate beings for their selfless gifts—for their devotion to your well-being and happiness?

Here is what we think they would answer: Be good to yourself. Without fail. Without exception. Without question. This space in your home is where you begin the journey of compassionate living by accepting compassion and affirming your worthiness.

All of these beings—humans, saints, teachers, Divine Beings— want you to believe you are worthy of space. Of breathing room.

A Final Note:
Embracing the Sacred
Messiness of Life

By now you've been inspired to declutter your home and heart. You've seen that there is a vast field of possibility open in your life, blossoming with the flowers of spirit—happiness, ease, and freedom. The path to that open place leads straight through the very place that you live. Perhaps you have already begun your decluttering and you're feeling that powerful Divine light shining within this work. You are thinking, *I have this. I am going to create a perfectly clear home and a perfectly clear heart.*

Slow down, intrepid declutterer. We love your energy and we celebrate your inspired movement toward creating breathing room in your life, but let's get one thing straight: there is no such thing as perfectly clear—not on any plane of your existence. Not physically, mentally, emotionally, or spiritually. Nor should there be.

Cluttering objects, thoughts, emotions, and spiritual blockages will make their way into our lives. Whether it's junk mail that literally arrives on your doorstep, or cheap plastic toys that come home from kids' birthday parties; whether they are distracted thoughts that draw you away from the beauty of the moment, petty resentments that arise at work or at home, or worldly temptations away from your Divine nature—clutter has its way of sneaking in and making itself at home. Clutter will find its way into your life. Again and again.

Letting Go of Perfection

The point of this work is not to eliminate clutter. To eliminate clutter is to eliminate life itself. Life brings us clutter. It lays it at our feet and asks, "What do you really need in your life to thrive and to feel connected to your humanity and your Source?" It is a gift to be able to choose. Knowing what we need and love, accepting it, and embracing it is a profound gift we humans have been given: the gift of discernment and self-determination. So eliminating clutter completely (if such a thing were even possible) eliminates our power of discernment and self-determination. Getting rid of all clutter would eliminate our ability to choose what we are going to create and make of our lives. It would eliminate powerful spiritual lessons.

Through these lessons, we grow in heart, soul, and spirit. It's how our hearts and spirits become meaningfully woven together with the hearts and spirits of others. It may seem trivial, but to be able to look at a little plastic car that your child could not care less about, or a bitter disappointment that is holding you back from seeing the wealth of possibilities in your future, and know *I do not need this is my life*—that means you know what your life is about. Each choice to let go is a way of saying: *This is not important to me. This will not help me to grow as a human being and to make good on the Divine contract I was sent to this earth to fulfill.* That decision is not the least bit trivial. It is huge! We need to encounter clutter in our lives to be able to say it.

Decluttering is an exercise in knowing intuitively what you deeply value and making sure what you value is never far from the surface. Decluttering as a spiritual practice allows you to constantly uncover and discover what is deeply meaningful, moving, and valuable in your life. It reminds you what matters most in life. Whenever you remove clutter from your home or your heart, you are meant to have a smiling moment of realization. Now, you will be able to say to yourself, the world, and your Creator, "Yes! This is what matters. This is what is meaningful. This is what I am here for."

So don't think, *I am going to declutter once and for all!* Why would you want to do that? You would be missing out on such a huge spiritual opportunity.

Keep Up the Good Work

Stay with it. Some days will be easier than others. Some days, you will make progress. Other days, you will see none at all. This is the nature of a spiritual path. The most important part is to keep walking.

And when in doubt, remember this, beloveds:

Compassion. Compassion. Compassion.

This is what we must return to. Compassion is the core of creating breathing room in the first place, is it not? It is the place we return to again and again to offer ourselves the loving-kindness and forgiveness we are worthy of, simply because we are children of the Universe, beloveds of the Divine—made of equal parts mud and stardust. Light is our nature, but mess is also our nature. We transgress in order to be forgiven.

Keep a place open in your heart that you can always return to, knowing that compassion and loving-kindness are awaiting your return. You are never more than a breath away from your breathing room.

As we close, we offer this blessing for every courageous declutterer:

May you always find what's most sacred within arm's reach. May you hold it with gratitude, knowing it is a grace and a gift. May happiness be out in the open, shining its light on your life. May you find breathing room wherever you go in life and offer that sense of spaciousness and freedom wherever you go. May love always sit on the mantel of your heart, for all to see.

May the heart of your home warm everyone who enters it.

May the home that is your heart be a blessing to everyone you meet.

Acknowledgments

This book represents the hard work and loving commitment of so many treasured people in our lives.

Our heartfelt thanks to the courageous declutterers whose stories appear in this book. You allowed us into your homes and your hearts, and we know that your stories will serve as a blessing and encouragement to all who read them. There were many others who spoke to us about their clutter whose stories do not appear in this book. We thank you as well for your willingness to open your lives to us and for informing our understanding of the profound connection between heart and home.

Thank you to Stephany Evans of FinePrint Literary Management for immediately seeing the promise in this book and supporting it with such enthusiasm. And thanks to Becky Vinter for helping us join creative forces with the publisher that was precisely the perfect fit for us.

And how fortunate we feel to have found ourselves in the midst of such a supportive family environment at Beyond Words. From the start, your excitement about this project has buoyed us. You've made this rigorous process a joy. Thank you to Anna Noak for your regular check-ins throughout the writing phase and your support and guidance. And to the editing team—Lindsay Brown, Emmalisa Sparrow, Gretchen Stelter, Claire Foster, and Linda Meyer—who decluttered the manuscript, helping it speak its message with a crystal clear voice. We are so grateful to you for lending your eyes, your hearts, and your mad skills to make *Breathing Room* a joyful read.

We are ever grateful to the venerable Thich Nhat Hanh, whose lesson regarding the necessity of creating a breathing room inspired this book.

To our families.

Lauren would like to tell her family: Y'all are the soul of my soul. That alone is enough to give thanks for eternally. But there's more. Thank you for all the hours you spent over family dinners, hanging out in the living room, and sitting in the van listening to me spin out ideas for this book. Thank you to Mira, Alec, Tamar, and Askar for keeping up your end of the chores and cooking on the days that writing and editing were my sole focus and for being willing to declutter our own home to create our own breathing room and showing that it can be done. And that breathing room does create miracles in home and heart. To Jamie, thank you for being my partner in everything and for allowing your heart to be my constant home.

Melva would like to say to her beloved son, Jeffrey "JB" Brown: My dearest awakened king-man-child, from the moment I first held you, you have indeed shown me that I was born to fly. Thank you for being my coadventurer in life and for being my soul's true teacher. In the past two years, you have allowed me to let go of so much clutter in my heart, and we have gained so much together in the process. The light of your presence is a reminder to me of the Divinity within us all.